# The
# Social
# Dimension
# of
# 1992

# THE
# SOCIAL
# DIMENSION
## OF
# 1992

## Europe Faces a New EC

### BEVERLY SPRINGER

PRAEGER

New York
Westport, Connecticut
London

**Library of Congress Cataloging-in-Publication Data**

Springer, Beverly.
     The social dimension of 1992 : Europe faces a new EC / Beverly
Springer.
        p.  cm.
    Includes bibliographical references and index.
    ISBN 0-275-94182-5 (pbk.)
     1. European Economic Community—Social policy.  2. Social
security—European Economic Community countries.  3. Labor policy—
European Economic Community countries.  4. Public welfare—European
Economic Community countries.  5. Europe—Economic integration—
Social aspects.  6. Europe 1992.  I. Title.
HN380.5.A8S7   1992b
303.4'094—dc20      91-22362

British Library Cataloguing in Publication Data is available.

A hardcover edition of *The Social Dimension of 1992* is
available from the Greenwood Press imprint of Greenwood
Publishing Group, Inc. (Contributions in Labor Studies,
Number 38; ISBN 0-313-27400-2).

Library of Congress Catalog Card Number: 91-22362
ISBN: 0-275-94182-5

First published in 1992

Praeger Publishers, One Madison Avenue, New York, NY, 10010
An imprint of Greenwood Publishing Group, Inc.

Printed in the United States of America

The paper used in this book complies with the
Permanent Paper Standard issued by the National
Information Standards Organization (Z39.48-1984).

10 9 8 7 6 5 4 3 2 1

*To*
*Hazel Tanner Carr and Lee Springer*
*with love and respect*

# Contents

# Preface

The 1992 initiative of the European Community is a major economic event. Many books and articles have been written explaining the importance of the initiative and its relevance for the international economy. The economic policies contained in the initiative are now being implemented with broad popular support. The economic policies were outlined in the White Paper on Completing the Internal Market in 1985 (CEC 1985b). Three years later, the Commission of the European Community issued another document containing a set of proposed social policies which is to form the second pillar of the 1992 initiative. The proposal, which is called the *Social Dimension of the Internal Market*, has had a much more mixed reception than the economic policies. Some important political and business leaders oppose the addition of social policies to an economic initiative. Their goal is the single internal market. Other equally influential leaders argue that the social policies are necessary if the 1992 initiative is going to be more than an exercise in market liberalization. Their goal is European integration.

The primary purpose of the 1992 initiative is to create a single market comprised of 320 million affluent consumers. This should revitalize the economy and make European firms competitive in the global economy. However, the 320 million consumers are also citizens and voters in the twelve member states of the European Community (EC). They must be convinced that they will benefit from a more powerful EC and a single internal market. Many of the citizens are also employees who may find that their work situation is vastly altered by the creation of the single market. The successful implementation of the initiative then is directly linked to the short-term social consequences of the formation of the single internal market. The social dimension is designed to ameliorate those consequences.

The European Community has had very little impact on the daily life of ordinary Europeans. National governments continue to be the providers of social assistance and protection. Now, however, that role of national governments is threatened by the creation of the single internal market. Capital can flow to the country with the weakest laws and the least costly social policies. The proposals of the Social Dimension will protect Europeans from the loss of their national programs by expanding the responsibility of the EC to establish European norms. Increasingly, Europeans will look to the EC for policies of immediate concern to them. The Community will become a reality in the daily life of Europeans.

The subject of the book is the social dimension of the 1992 initiative. The book deals with both the substance and the politics of the policy. The topic is set within the context of the developments leading to the 1992 initiative. It explains both the relevance and the controversial aspects of the proposed social policies for the future of European integration. The proponents of the proposal state that it will have important consequences not only for employees in the European Community but also for the future of European integration. The European Community will provide rights for employees that are unknown in the legal system of the United States. In the process, the EC will gain authority and the sphere of action of member governments will be confined. Many business leaders and politicians fear this development and charge that it is a distortion of the original 1992 program.

The book is designed for two different groups of readers. Persons interested in international management or international human resource management need to understand the extent to which policies of the European Community are changing the environment for international business in Europe. The book contains descriptions of major developments in employment policies. It also places the developments within the context of European values and history so that the reader can understand the relevance of the policies. The author hopes that business readers will obtain a more realistic and moderate picture of the Social Dimension proposal than is sometimes provided in business literature.

The book is also designed for students of politics for whom the first chapters will provide a quick review of the history and organization of the European Community. The remaining chapters provide an examination of current developments in social policy in the European Community.

The information is based on extensive use of primary sources and numerous interviews carried on in Brussels over the past decade. The rationale for the Social Dimension is based, in large part, on functionalist assumptions regarding the process of European integration. The findings presented in the book provide the basis for renewed consideration of functionalism and neofunctionalism in the analysis of the European Community. The theoretical discussion in this book, however, is limited since the primary purpose of the book is to provide the reader with an understanding of major new policies in the European Community.

As everyone knows, events in Europe continue to occur with a speed that surpasses even the most diligent scholar supplied with the latest in high-tech research tools. The material in the book is current at the moment of writing. The formation of policies should continue along lines indicated in the book. The European Community is in a dynamic period and continues to move rapidly toward objectives set in the 1980s. So far, developments in eastern Europe have not deflected the European Community from those objectives. However, a change in major variables such as a significant decline in the current economic health in Western Europe or a huge influx of refugees from the East would, undoubtedly, affect the evolution of policy in the European Community.

# Acknowledgments

I would like to acknowledge the help that many people in the Commission have given me over the past ten years. Three people, in particular, gave generously of their time and their knowledge. They are Ivor Roberts, Chris Docksey, and Pauline Jackson.

I also want to thank Zeddie Landam of the American Graduate School of International Management for using his red pen so freely to correct my manuscript.

# The
# Social
# Dimension
# of
# 1992

# Chapter 1

# An Introduction to the European Community: Its Institutions and Policies

We are witnessing the transformation of the European Community from its modest origins in postwar Europe into a confident actor in the world. The scope of its authority ranges from the determination of acceptable noise levels for lawn mowers sold in the twelve member states of the European Community to the formulation of western policy toward Eastern Europe. The European Community is an economic powerhouse with growing political ambitions. The authority of the European Community to make laws and policies increasingly extends into areas formerly reserved for governments of sovereign states. The European Community is much more than an international organization, but it is not yet—and may never be—the government of an integrated Europe.

The impetus for the transformation of the European Community comes from an initiative usually referred to simply by the year 1992. When national governments failed to solve the economic difficulties confronting Western Europe in the 1980s, certain political leaders and businesspersons joined together to revitalize the European Community. Their objective was to sweep away the barriers which continued to divide the markets of the twelve member countries and to create a single, internal market by the year 1992. They accepted the fact that the EC would have to become more powerful and efficient in order to meet their objective. The initiative which these political leaders and businesspersons set in motion progressed with surprising speed. By the end of the decade, politicians could proclaim that the process was irreversible. Media campaigns informed the public. 1992, coupled with an attractive blue and gold flag and a stirring EC anthem, could be seen and heard from Greece to Denmark. 1992 is no longer a symbol only for political leaders and businesspersons. It is a broadly accepted fact, and many Europeans are now beginning to consider the ramifications of the change.

In order to understand the significance of the transformation taking place in Western Europe, one needs first to consider briefly the earlier history of the EC and also the institutions which carry on the work of the EC. The EC was formed in the 1950s by a small elite. It was reformed in the 1980s by another small elite. Ordinary Europeans were present neither at the formation nor at the reformation. They were not much involved nor much affected by what went on in the EC in the decades between the two events either. In the early years, the EC was sometimes called the businessmen's Europe. Its policies primarily dealt with issues of concern to large businesses. To a certain extent, the EC can still be called a businessmen's Europe. Business people are the most immediate beneficiaries of 1992; however, a growing number of people now recognize that the EC cannot remain the preserve of an elite and the benefactor of a single group. The EC can only have the power which it needs if it is given legitimacy by ordinary Europeans. To obtain that legitimacy, the EC must not only provide some benefits to its citizens, it must also have some emotional attraction for them as well. The leaders of the EC are now formulating a number of policies, known as the *Social Dimension of the Internal Market*, that should help them create those benefits and that attraction. The Social Dimension is controversial, but its proponents hope that it will result in an EC that is much more than a businessmen's Europe.

The EC took root in the years following World War II when European leaders sought the means to restore Europe and to secure its future (Mowat 1973). National governments had been discredited by their failure to cure the depression of the 1930s or to prevent the outbreak of a second major war; however, no acceptable alternative was found in the immediate postwar years. Traditional international organizations had failed in the past, and few political leaders were ready to abandon entirely national sovereignty for some form of supranational government. Then, in the 1950s, three new organizations were created which seemed to offer a promising balance between national sovereignty and supranationalism. Those organizations were called communities to designate that they were more than international organizations but not yet supranational entities. Only six countries (France, Italy, the Federal Republic of Germany, Belgium, The Netherlands, and Luxembourg) were willing to sign the treaties establishing the communities. Each signatory agreed to give up a small portion of sovereignty to the new entities for limited and practical purposes.

The three communities were the European Coal and Steel Community (1952), the European Atomic Energy Community (1958), and the European Economic Community (1958). Each had a set of governing institutions and a basic treaty which defined its powers. Within the narrow confines of its treaty, each community had sovereign powers to make and enforce law. The new entities were practical and dealt with matters that aroused little public interest. Some Europeans hoped, however, that the communities would be the building blocks for an integrated Europe (Pryce 1987).

The European Economic Community (EEC) became the most important of the three communities. The Treaty of Rome, which established the EEC, states that its basic objective is to create an economic area in which labor, capital, services, and goods circulate freely in order to provide for greater economic prosperity and a higher standard of living for all persons residing in the area. The six economies of the founding members were to be joined in a common market without internal barriers to trade and with common external barriers to trade. The institutions of the EEC were given the power to make the policies necessary for that objective. The governments of the member states retained the power to make all other economic policies.

The years after the formation of the three communities were good years for Western Europe. Living standards and economic growth rates reached record levels. National governments enacted programs which improved the quality of life for average Europeans. The communities settled into a rather mundane existence. The EEC was able to implement its initial programs ahead of schedule. It overcame an agricultural crisis in the 1960s and continued to work on the creation of a common market. European firms and American multinational corporations benefitted from EEC policies, but EEC policies hardly affected the daily life of Europeans. Ordinary Europeans found little to praise or blame in the activities of the communities.

In 1969, the institutions of the three communities were merged to form the European Community (EC); however, the original treaties still defined the powers which the institutions exercised in each of the three areas. A single set of institutions governed with the powers provided by the original treaties. Those treaties served as the framework or constitution of the EC.

The EC added three new members in the 1970s. They were the United Kingdom, Denmark, and Ireland. The policies of the EC also expanded in that decade to include social, environmental, and monetary policies. The EC became a significant, but still not highly visible, part of the economic life of Western Europe.

The rather steady evolution of the EC was interrupted by two major developments. One was the addition of the three new members in 1972. Policy making became more difficult when it involved reconciling differences among nine governments rather than six. The integration of the United Kingdom was especially difficult. Its economy, based on ties with former colonies, was not easily aligned with the more rapidly growing economies of the original members. In addition, its legal system differed significantly from that of continental countries. The writing of EC laws became more complex. The entire decision-making process became tedious.

The other major development which interrupted the evolution of the EC was the economic recession of the 1970s. It more severely affected the EC than the United States because of a higher dependence on imported oil. Escalating oil prices devastated the balance of payments of European countries and squeezed profits of European industries. Profits were already under pressure from rising labor costs. The result was a recession, growing unemployment, and severe economic difficulties for many governments. National governments tried to ease the situation by turning inward and shutting out competition from other countries. The EC was not able to maintain the momentum toward integration in the face of growing nationalism, even though it had moments of vitality and continued to add new members. Greece joined in 1980. Spain and Portugal joined in 1986, but for many Europeans, the EC appeared to be irrelevant to the problems confronting them.

From 1973 to 1985, Western Europe not only experienced major economic problems but also experienced an even more devastating loss of confidence (Braun et al. 1983). Western Europeans had developed a lifestyle which depended on economic growth. Their governments had also, but their industries could no longer sustain that growth. European firms lost their leadership in high technology to the Americans and Japanese. They lost their mass consumer markets to new competitors from the Third World. The situation bred "Europessimism." Many feared that the economic miracle was over and that they would have to accept a lifestyle of shabby gentility.

Looking back from the vantage point of the 1990s, it may appear obvious that leaders would turn to the EC for solutions to the problems in Europe when different national policies had failed to alleviate the situation; however, the EC did not look very promising in the early

1980s. It appeared locked in chronic disputes over agriculture and budget. Its leaders engaged in futile attempts to standardize such products as chocolate and beer, arousing the anger and disgust of consumers in member states. The press pictured the EC as an oversized bureaucracy staffed by overpaid, high-living, and underworked Eurocrats. Even supporters of the EC were discouraged by its inability to take action on important issues. A proposed policy could take ten years to pass through the cumbersome decision-making process, and many proposals survived the procedure only to disappear without a trace when they reached the Council of Ministers. The policies that did gain acceptance were frequently so battered by the process that they had lost much of their original significance. A few persons did perceive the possibilities in the EC and set about in the early 1980s to reform it in order to make it the engine to pull Europe out of the doldrums of the time.

The work of the EC is carried on through a complex process which involves four major institutions, numerous European agencies, political parties, and interest groups as well as the governments of the member states (Budd and Jones 1989). The four major institutions are the Council of Ministers, the Commission, the Parliament and the Court of Justice. They were designed by the framers of the treaties to carry out limited government functions of law making, law implementing, and law enforcing. They were also designed to reflect the balance between the authority of the member states and the limited supranational authority of the EC. By the 1980s, each of the institutions had obvious weaknesses which obstructed effectiveness. The original role of each of the institutions is explained briefly in the paragraphs that follow as well as some of the weaknesses. Then the changes set in motion by the Single European Act will be discussed. References are given for those readers who want more information.

The Council of Ministers is the voice of the member states and it is the primary law-making institution of the EC. Cabinet ministers from the governments of the member states participate in the work of the Council. The participants are primarily national political leaders, so the Council is the least "European" of the four institutions. Participants jealously protect their spheres of national authority and their own perceptions of national interests. Throughout most of the history of the EC, each member state had a veto on important proposals which came before the Council. Given the concerns of the participants and the different perceptions of national interests, no one is surprised that the Council has become the graveyard of EC initiatives.

The presidency of the Council rotates every six months (de Bassompierre 1988). It is held by a member state, not an individual. Each government attempts to make its own imprint during its tenure in the presidency and to advance certain favored proposals, especially during meetings of the European Council. These are special meetings of the Council attended by the heads of government of the member states. One meeting of the European Council always takes place in the country that holds the presidency. Those meetings are a time of intense politicking and many have gone down in history for their successes or failures. A good example occurred in 1989 when the French held the presidency. The final Council meeting of the French presidency was held amidst great grandeur in Paris where the celebration of the French bicentenary was in full swing. President François Mitterrand endorsed ambitious proposals to advance European integration. He also sought to promote the social dimension of 1992, as did the subsequent Spanish presidency. The role played by President Mitterrand, no doubt, reflected his own convictions about European integration, but it also undoubtedly served to enhance his own domestic political stature. Statesmanship and politics are closely linked when a government holds the presidency of the Council.

The Council may be the most famous of the EC institutions, but the Commission is the most pervasive and the most "European." It has a wide range of responsibilities. It drafts proposals for policies. It watches over the implementation of EC policies. It is the guardian of the treaties and it even has limited police powers, most particularly in the enforcing of competition policy. It is a large bureaucracy which today has outgrown its home in the Berlaymont building in Brussels. At the top of the Commission are seventeen commissioners who are appointed for four-year terms. (Each of the five largest member states sends two commissioners. Each of the other member states sends one.) During their appointments they are full-time Europeans and not the instructed delegates of member states. The commissioners oversee some 9,000 civil servants. Each commissioner is responsible for a specific sector and one commissioner is designated the President. The commissioner who has responsibility for the sector dealt with in this book is Madame Vasso Papandreou. She was proposed as a commissioner in 1989 by the Greek government. She was made responsible for employment and social policies. She became the "boss" of the civil servants who work in DG V. (DG refers to directorate general. The Commission is divided into 23 DGs or functional divisions. DG V deals with policies relating to employment, social affairs, education, training, and human resources.)

The effectiveness of the Commission was limited by its lack of a political base and its weak leadership throughout much of its history. The Commission had little leverage to force the Council to act. The Commission could spend years in drafting a proposal which the Council could then allow to disappear by never scheduling the proposal for consideration on its agenda. The Commission remained faceless and remote from Europeans. Individual commissioners were too frequently persons who had outlived their political careers in their member states, so were sent off to Brussels as a type of golden handshake.

In recent years the balance of power between the Council and the Commission has shifted somewhat in favor of the Commission. Jacques Delors, the President of the Commission, has revitalized the image of the Commission. He did not leave Paris in order to become a faceless Eurocrat in Brussels. He has used the Commission's power of initiative to promote significant new initiatives. He is a highly visible actor in the new European politics surrounding the 1992 initiative. His selection to serve a second term on the Commission has also served to enhance its power vis-à-vis the Council with its rotating presidency.

The European Parliament is less powerful than either the Council or the Commission but its importance has grown in recent years (Palmer 1981). Its 518 members live the life of political gypsies with ties to a political constituency in a member state, membership in a European political party, attendance in plenary sessions in Strasbourg, and frequent meetings in Luxembourg and Brussels. The European Parliament should not be compared to a national parliament, even though its members are elected on political party tickets just as are members of national parliaments. In the early days its members were not even elected. The Parliament existed largely to give a democratic gloss to the work of the EC, but few were fooled into thinking that it had any real power. Until recently, its legislative power has been minimal. The importance of Parliament began to increase in 1979 when direct elections to Parliament started, but it still functioned in the relative obscurity of Strasbourg. Its main activity was to write opinions on Commission proposals before their consideration by the Council. The Council was not required to respect those opinions. Indeed, it took a ruling of the Court to force the Council at least to wait for the opinion of Parliament before acting (Kirchner and Williams 1983).

Generally, Parliament is the ally of the Commission. Both institutions are more "European" than the Council. Members of the European Parliament from most political parties tend to support European issues more strongly than do their party counterparts in national parliaments.

Commissioners work closely with committees of the Parliament when they are considering a proposal. It is not unusual for individuals in Parliament to express more rapport with persons in the Commission than with persons in the Council, even when the latter are from the same political party. The sense of "Europeanism" is the glue which links the Commission and Parliament.

The Court of Justice is the fourth institution of the EC (Lasok and Bridge 1987: 248–86). It is composed of thirteen judges who are appointed for six-year terms by agreement among the member states. Within the limits of the authority granted by the original treaties, the Court has always had real power. Its rulings must be respected in the member states, and it is the final arbiter in interpreting Community law. Through the years it has quietly laid the basis for a broad interpretation of treaty powers and provided an impressive body of judicial opinion which has quite consistently upheld the right of EC institutions to act in areas not clearly defined as falling within the authority of the EC. The main weakness that troubled the Court in the 1980s was its inability to cope with an escalating workload.

Until the 1980s, the four institutions worked together in a policy-making process which, for most topics, was relatively simple. The Commission had the authority to initiate proposals. The Parliament studied them and wrote an opinion. The Council accepted them by a voting arrangement that generally allowed any member state to veto a proposal which was contrary to the national interest. The Court ruled on legal questions relating to the policies. The process was adequate as long as the topics were not controversial and no need existed for speedy action. The policies which emerged from the process often were minimalist and did little to edge the EC down the road toward greater integration. They seldom excited much public interest.

The institutions of the EC and the policy-making process were both changed significantly in 1985 with the Single European Act (SEA) (Lodge 1989). One may say that without the SEA there could be no 1992 initiative. The SEA is a treaty that was ratified by all the member states and serves as an amendment to the basic treaties of the EC. It provides for a more efficient policy-making process and also lays the basis for wider policy-making authority in the EC.

The EC was always a compromise between persons who envisioned a united states of Europe and persons who accepted only the degree of integration necessary for certain limited objectives. By the 1980s, both groups had cause to believe that another step toward greater integration was needed. Reform efforts began in a variety of places and among quite diverse groups. The 1992 initiative is one consequence of those efforts and will be dealt with in the next chapter. The other important consequence is the Single European Act. The two are closely intertwined, and probably neither could exist without the other.

The Single European Act went into effect in 1987 following its ratification by all the member states of the EC. The treaty reforms the institutions of the EC and expands their sphere of competence. It also formalizes greater cooperation among the member governments on international politics.

The Council, the Commission, and the Parliament all were involved in the creation of the SEA. Participants came from political parties across the European political spectrum. All agreed on the need to reform the EC even though they disagreed on the amount of change needed. The Parliament made the most ambitious proposal with a draft treaty which would have replaced the existing treaties. The work of the Dooge Committee, which was established by the European Council, was more cautious. Each government had a representative on the committee, so its work was broadly acceptable when the governments met in an intergovernmental conference in 1985 to draft the treaty (Pryce 1987).

The SEA extends the use of the "qualified majority" voting in the Council. Under such voting, each member state has a block of votes depending on its relative size and importance. France, Germany, Italy, and the United Kingdom have ten votes each; Spain has eight; Belgium, The Netherlands, Greece, and Portugal have five each; Denmark and Ireland have three; and Luxembourg has two. It takes fifty-four votes out of the possible total of seventy-six for a proposal to be passed.

The issue of voting was controversial in the discussions leading to the writing of the treaty. As a compromise, the SEA stipulates, in separate articles, when qualified majority voting shall be used. Unanimity remains the rule for sensitive issues such as tax policies. The treaty could not always make precise distinctions, so it left unclear, in the case of some social and environmental proposals for example, whether unanimity or "qualified majority" voting is required. The Court will probably need to decide a number of disputes. In general, qualified majority may be used for proposals dealing with the formation of the internal market. The new voting procedure is a major reason why the enactment of the proposals necessary for the 1992 initiative have gone forward with such remarkable speed.

The use of qualified majority not only expedites action in the Council, it also opens up a niche for more political coalition building to go on among the Commission, the Parliament, and the Council. The Commission only needs the votes of at least seven of the members to have its proposal accepted in the Council, but the Council must be unanimous in order to change a proposal of the Commission. Also, governments who consistently obstruct a proposal lose their clout when they can be outvoted. The Commission has less need today to keep British concerns constantly in mind when drafting legislation than it had before the SEA. The politics of obstruction used to work well for Margaret Thatcher but now it only leaves the British isolated on many important issues.

The SEA provided for no direct reform of the Commission despite many proposals in the original discussions, but it did expand the policy areas subject to EC authority. (For example, some reformers—especially in the Parliament—want the Parliament to select the Commission in order to enhance the democratic authority of the Commission as well as the power of the Parliament.) Under the leadership of Jacques Delors, the Commission has acted quickly to widen its field of activity with new initiatives for monetary policy, social policy, and the environment. The Commission has also been the moving force leading to another intergovernmental conference to consider further steps toward European integration. One of the issues before the conference is the size of the Commission. As the Commission has grown through the addition of new member states it has become more difficult to form a working group and it has also become more difficult to divide responsibilities for the DGs. The expected addition of new states will seriously exacerbate the problem.

The Parliament gained power through the SEA in several ways. In regard to policy making, the Parliament cannot be overlooked as easily as in the past. Ten articles in the SEA stipulate that the "cooperation procedure" must be used when the EC is considering a proposal drafted under the authority of any one of them. The cooperation procedure is used most frequently when matters dealing with the establishment of the internal market are under consideration, but it also includes some proposals dealing with social policy. When a proposal falls under that procedure, the Parliament must be consulted twice. The Council can only ignore changes inserted by Parliament during its second consultation if the Council members are unanimous. In itself, the new procedure does not give the Parliament significant new powers; however, it does open the opportunity for clever members of the Parliament to publicize their position and to challenge the Council to go against public opinion as expressed through the Parliament.

A recent study on the Parliament indicates that members of Parliament are using the cooperation procedure effectively (Corbett 1989). Members urge the Commission to draft proposals so that they fall under provisions of the SEA that require use of the cooperation procedure. The study also finds that the two-reading procedure has strengthened the bargaining strength of the Parliament with the Council. When the majority of the Council supports a proposal requiring the cooperation, that majority must either win the unanimous agreement of all Council members or reach a mutually satisfactory agreement with the Parliament.

According to the same study, the Parliament dealt with fifty-three proposals covered by the cooperation procedure during the first eighteen months following its implementation. The Parliament accepted seven of them and amended forty-six. The Commission accepted 462 of 603 amendments proposed by the Parliament. When forty-one of the proposals came to the Parliament after the Council had reached an agreement on them, the Parliament accepted twenty-two of them, amended eighteen and rejected one (which the Council then failed to adopt by the required unanimous vote) (Corbett 1989: 364–68).

## CONCLUSION

The EC has been part of the political and economic life of Europe for almost four decades. Its history has been marked by eras of vitality and periods when the EC has been almost irrelevant to developments of the time. Today it is rejuvenated by a new and attractive mandate known simply as 1992. It has also been given the tools to implement that mandate by the SEA. The rejuvenation has made the EC a much more visible and important actor in political and economic life in Europe in the 1990s than it had been since its nadir in the 1970s.

The EC is neither a supranational government nor a traditional international organization. It has elements of sovereignty but its members retain sovereignty as well. It is customary now to speak of "pooled sovereignty" in reference to the scope of authority of the EC, that depends upon its basic treaties for its grant to power and the formation of its institutions. It has law-making authority within the sphere set by the treaties but the authority must always be exercised through a complex interaction with the member states.

The institutions of the EC have an apparent similarity with those found in national governments but important differences exist. The institutions of the EC reflect its hybrid nature, combining the voices of Europe with the voices of the member states. The Commission, the Parliament, and the Court all have a marked "European" view but the Council continues to reflect national interests and it is the Council that has the ultimate law-making authority.

The formal decision-making process of the EC is rather straightforward. The Commission initiates, the Parliament tries to shape the proposal in the interest of the "people" of Europe, and the Council decides. The SEA reformed the process in order to make it more efficient and more democratic.

The reality of decision making is less tidy but much more interesting than the formal outlines indicate. Interest groups, consultants, political parties, and the media all get involved. Some proposals arouse intense pressures and others slip by in relative obscurity. Since the EC set to work on the 1992 initiative, the whole decision-making process has become fraught with political pressures. This is especially true in regard to the social dimension of the 1992 initiative as will be examined in Chapter 5, which deals with the politics of the social dimension.

The EC has been transformed from an obscure organization of the postwar era that devised policies of interest to only a relative few in Western Europe, to the EC that has ambitious objectives. The relevance of its work reaches well beyond the offices of international businesses. The institutions of the EC, which were designed in the earlier era, have been reformed to serve the objectives of today, even though those institutions do not conform to generally held norms of western democratic government. The citizens of the member states are still distant from the decision-making process, but the success of the current ambitious objectives of the EC now require democratic legitimacy. As the EC moves down the road toward economic integration, the scope of policies reach out further and further and affect more people. The EC cannot be perceived to have a democratic deficit by Europeans, so a social dimension has been added to the current 1992 initiative, and the institutions of the EC must be perceived as legitimate by Europeans. The politics and policies of the social dimension may well determine how far the 1992 initiative will move the EC toward integration.

*Chapter 2*

# The 1992 Initiative: Its Genesis, Scope, and Purpose

"1992" was the marketing coup of the 1980s. When that simple logo started to appear in publicity campaigns, Europeans were in their darkest stages of Europessimism. The effect of 1992 was amazing. People began to believe that an escape was possible from the economic problems which seemed to defy solution. The genius of the 1992 initiative is its simplicity and the confidence which it inspires. People were provided with a schedule of steps to take, starting immediately and finishing on December 31, 1992. On January 1, 1993, a new Europe will be born (Bieber et al. 1988; Calingaert 1988).

The initiative is working. Change is occurring at many levels. The importance of the transformation is difficult to overestimate. Anyone interested in Western Europe today needs to have a complete grasp of the 1992 initiative. The task of this chapter is to examine the genesis, scope, and purpose of the initiative in order to understand fully what is taking place. When the full extent of the relevance of the 1992 initiative is understood, then the question which inevitably follows is, "Will 1992 result in an EC which is still essentially a businessman's Europe, or will the initiative force the EC to expand its scope and become the foundation of a people's Europe?" The remainder of this book will be used to answer that question.

## THE GENESIS OF THE 1992 INITIATIVE

The norms which apply to the European political economy differ significantly from those found in the United States. The assumptions of laissez-faire economics have never enjoyed the broad acceptance in Europe which they have in the United States. When Western Europe began to rebuild after World War II, governments played an important role in guiding economic plans and assuring social safeguards for employees. Even in the Federal Republic of Germany (FRG), the famous social market economy provides employees with extensive social security, including health insurance. The bill is paid largely by German firms. Governments are also important owners of enterprises in most countries, most notably in France and Italy, but government ownership also exists in the FRG.

Such mixed economies were largely unquestioned until the 1970s. When the recession hit, however, everyone searched for the guilty party. Those who blamed governments found important supporting facts. Governments absorbed increasingly larger percentages of the gross domestic product (GDP) in all countries. The nationalized industries in many countries were too frequently guided by political rather than economic criteria. The regulatory state hemmed in the private sector and stifled innovation. The costs imposed by government policies made European firms uncompetitive and social protections hindered the ability of managers to use employees in cost-effective ways. Flexibility, deregulation, and privatization became rallying cries for critics of the existing system.

Not all critics believed that governments were the culprits. They noted that the evidence was not clear cut. No exact correlation could be drawn between the percentage of a GDP absorbed by a government and the vitality of an economy. Those critics blamed the private sector, where they charged that managers were more interested in profits than innovation and more interested in their status than listening to ideas from their employees. These critics believed not that government policies, per se, were wrong but rather that government had the wrong policies.

Each of the two groups of critics found a champion in a government holding office in the early 1980s. The Conservative government of Margaret Thatcher launched an economic program more firmly based on the assumptions of laissez-faire economics than any in postwar European history. The vigor and conviction of her leadership attracted a following which spread well beyond her island kingdom. Thatcherism, coupled with Reaganism, appeared to many to be the solution for what ailed Europe.

Across the channel in France, the Socialist government gambled on a "dash for growth" in which the government nationalized firms and pumped public capital into them. Public policies were changed to redistribute wealth and power away from traditional groups and toward employees. The French government quickly learned, however, that it could not, as a country so closely linked to the EC and the global economy, follow expansionary policies when those policies were firmly opposed by holders of capital and its major trading partners. A balance-of-payments crisis and an investment strike by private holders of capital soon sent danger signals which the French socialists, always more pragmatic than many foreign observers realized, heeded. France adopted a much attenuated form of Thatcherism which continued through the next two changes of government. Other governments also espoused privatization, deregulation, and budget restraint.

By 1983, economic thought in Western Europe generally held that the role of government in the economy needed to be reduced. The needs of private firms to be free of government intervention and to be more profitable became part of the accepted norms, and under those new norms, private firms became more assertive. Politicians listened carefully to their demands.

It is against the background described above that the 1992 initiative needs to be considered. The EC has never been isolated from the prevailing doctrines of the day. Despite its weak democratic structure, the EC has consistently responded to changing norms ranging from individual values, such as women's issues, to more theoretical concerns, such as the proper way to manage an economy. By 1983, flexibility was the buzz word in the halls of the Berlaymont where the Eurocrats draft EC policy. In that same year, the Parliament received a report which laid the blame for the chronic economic problems on the fragmentation of the European market and on the waste which resulted from restrictive national practices. The declarations of European summits held between 1982 and 1985 show an increasing sense of urgency among European leaders to revitalize the economy by clearing away constraints on the internal market. Clearly, the economic orthodoxy of the day was accepted inside the EC.

Two additional developments paved the way for the 1992 initiative. Leading industrialists in Western Europe had formed a group known as the Roundtable of European Industrialists. They discussed what conditions they needed in order to make their firms competitive in the global economy. They believed that American and Japanese firms benefitted from conditions which reduced their costs and allowed them to be more flexible than comparable European firms. The industrialists supported the economic liberalization of national governments but realized that European firms were still harmed by the smallness of their home markets.

One of the leaders of the Roundtable, Wisse Dekker, the head of Phillips, the Dutch multinational corporation, made several speeches promoting the idea that the EC should complete the internal market which had been promised in the original Treaty of Rome. Wisse Dekker is known and respected in Brussels, so his message was heard. In the jargon of the day, important business people told the EC that they needed the "critical mass" necessary to support the development and promotion of products to compete in the global economy and that the EC should take steps to create the appropriately large, domestic market.

The second essential development leading to the 1992 initiative was the arrival in Brussels of a new Commission in 1985. Two persons on that Commission were vital to the initiative, and they were a most unlikely pair. Jacques Delors, the president of the Commission, was a former finance minister in the French Socialist government. He is the ultimate French technocrat: intelligent, highly educated, and extremely confident. Lord Arthur Cockfield, the commissioner responsible for the internal market, was appointed by Margaret Thatcher, who, no doubt, thought that she was making a nice gesture for a respected, retired businessman. The French socialist and the British businessman became the framers of the 1992 initiative.

Jacques Delors wanted to revitalize the EC and decided that the most promising way would be to renew the effort to create a single market. The Council supported the idea and requested the Commission to prepare a paper outlining a program. The task fell to Lord Cockfield and the outcome was the famous White Paper on Completing the Internal Market, which was submitted to the European Council held in Milan in June 1985 (CEC 1985b). The White Paper is the bible of the 1992 initiative, and its acceptance by the European Council set the program in motion. The final step in legitimating the 1992 initiative was taken in the Single European Act, the new treaty that amended the Treaty of Rome. The treaty contains a reference to the completion of the internal market by 1992 and provides for the adoption of the necessary laws by a qualified majority vote in the Council.

## THE SCOPE OF THE 1992 INITIATIVE

The 1992 initiative, as outlined in the White Paper, was well designed to assure broad support in the 1980s. The tone is confident and optimistic. The body of the paper contains a succinct statement about the scope and justification for the program. The annex contains a timetable and a list of the approximately 300 measures needed to complete the internal market. The program appears realistic and nonthreatening. No expenditures are listed. No revolutionary statements about the transfer of sovereignty are made. Instead, the point is made that the EC is only doing what it is supposed to do under the Treaty of Rome. The proposal is simply to remove the physical, technical, and fiscal barriers to the internal market. It focuses on removing a cumbersome layer of national regulations instead of on creating a new supranational, regulatory state. Margaret Thatcher, as well as European industrialists, were able to support the proposal. Even labor unions could take comfort in the promise that unemployment would decline in the new, internal market.

The scope of the program is limited to the creation of the internal market through the elimination of barriers. Other policies, such as monetary integration and social policy, are mentioned only to the effect that they are beyond the confines of the program. Much attention is given to the need to eliminate the barrier created by national standards, an obscure topic to many people but a costly obstacle for EC firms who want to sell their products outside their national market. The problem of national borders is more visible, and people could appreciate how prices in the EC were increased because of high transportation costs resulting from delays at borders. The rest of the topics dealt with are equally diverse and more or less visible to the public; however, all fall under the scope set by the title of the White Paper.

The implementation of the program is designed to be progressive, with change steadily taking place until 1993. Most of the proposed changes are in the form of directives. A directive is one of the two major forms of EC law. It serves as a framework which requires every member state to enact a national law which fits within the framework. A directive sets parameters but allows for national differences. The process of implementing a directive is slow and uneven, as member governments act with different degrees of speed. When the directive is fully implemented, the individuals or firms affected by the directive deal directly with the national law rather than with the directive, so the implementation of the 1992 initiative is much subtler than the original perceptions of the proposal that seemed to imply a sudden uniform, and dramatic dawn of a new Europe on January 1, 1993.

## THE PURPOSE OF THE 1992 INITIATIVE

The primary purpose of the 1992 initiative is to make European firms competitive in the world economy and thereby revitalize the EC economy. The assumption is if that purpose is served, then other benefits will result, such as better jobs and wages. That assumption is so deeply imbedded in the document that almost no attention is given to possible negative consequences. Creating the internal market is the number one priority of the EC.

The widespread acceptance of the primary purpose gives the EC a mission and a prominence unmatched by any previous EC initiative. The commitment of the Commission to the success of 1992 is unquestioned. Even the drama in Eastern Europe has not been allowed to interrupt the program. The work has moved forward with amazing speed and the Council and the Parliament have not obstructed progress. The business community is generally happy with the changes, and public opinion supports the idea of greater economic integration.

The purpose of the 1992 initiative is in accord with the prevailing economic doctrines of the 1980s. Firms should be set free from the restrictions of national governments, and the market should be unfettered. Then recovery will follow, bringing with it solutions to many other problems in Europe. However, as the EC speeds toward the fulfillment of that purpose, some people inevitably begin to worry about the ramifications of the changes and even to question the assumptions on which the policy is based. One of the major worries is what happens to the people of Europe as they wait for the benefits to trickle down to them. Another is what assurances do they have that 1992 will work for them. If the economic purpose of 1992 does not offer any social benefits, then the necessary support could quickly disappear.

## CONCLUSION

By 1991 many of the features of the 1992 initiative were in place. The EC had important new laws to liberalize banking, the movement of capital, and insurances. Steps had been taken to open public procurement contracts to bidders throughout the EC. The new procedure on standards was making it easier for producers to design products for one large market rather than for twelve. Even the transportation sector was liberalizing under pressure from the EC. The European Council stated in its report of December 1990 that the main features of the large European market are now present (European Council, December 14 and 15, 1990).

Businesses responded to the promise of the internal market with a surge of investments and cross-border acquisitions. American and Japanese firms rushed into the EC in order to participate in the new market. A whole growth industry has been created to educate and service firms interested in 1992. Volumes have been written to inform business audiences of opportunities and risks. (See, for example, Quelch and Buzzell 1990; Williams, Teagan and Beneyto 1990.)

The EC has experienced strong economic growth and an improvement of most economic indicators which has added to the aura of success which surrounds the 1992 initiative. The EC has entered a positive cycle with confidence fueling activity and activity fueling reform, leading to more confidence. The EC now plays a leading role in international as well as European affairs. The stage appears set for a new initiative which is already underway with the establishment of a new intergovernmental conference to consider ways to further enhance the role of the EC in providing a more integrated and prosperous Europe. In economic and political terms, 1992 may be judged a success even before the year 1992 arrives. It remains to consider its success in providing a springboard for EC policy making in areas beyond those included in the internal market.

*Chapter 3*

---

# Europeans at Work: The Current Situation in the Member States

Employees in Europe have a large stake in the outcome of 1992.[*] Their frame of reference has always been their national economy and their national government. Their wages are generally determined by national agreements negotiated by their national labor unions. The social protections for employees have been provided by national governments. Now the formation of the internal market is changing the framework within which employees have operated. National agreements and national legal protections may have less force when employers operate within an EC market rather than within individual national markets. European employees have been promised that they will benefit from the formation of the internal market. They have also been promised that no regression will be allowed in the social conditions prevailing in the member states.

The purpose of this chapter is to provide the reader with an overview of current employment trends in Europe as well as a brief summary of national employment policies. The information forms the backdrop for an understanding of the objectives of the EC in adding a social dimension to the 1992 initiative.

---

[*] See appendix for charts of employment statistics.

## TRENDS IN EMPLOYMENT

Employees in the EC are accustomed to a standard of living and working conditions unmatched in most of the world. They are productive and they are organized with labor unions and political parties to promote their interests. Employee organizations are part of the establishment in most European countries. They use their political power to win legal rights for employees and to have a "fair share" of the national wealth. In recent years they have generally moderated their demands and complied with austerity measures enacted by national governments of both the right and the left; however, neither employees nor their organizations are willing to accept an erosion of living standards or working conditions, and few governments in the EC would want to confront employees on such issues.

Europeans may be the aristocrats in the world of work, but conditions are not uniform and stress arising from rapid change in the economy troubles all of them. While the German worker in a car factory enjoys six weeks of vacation, the worker in the underground economy of Naples exists in sweatshop conditions. While the Danish employee works with the latest technology, the Portuguese farm laborer uses the same tools as his grandfather. Throughout the EC, employees face conditions which add to the tensions of their daily lives. Women have made progress in the job market and have achieved relative pay equality, but they lack support in dealing with family and work responsibilities. Male employees have seen their status as skilled employees lost when whole categories of work have disappeared before the onslaught of modernization. Indeed, employees of almost every type and status find their jobs today more insecure and more unstable than in the past. Unemployment is a very real fear. Pressure to retrain and to relocate is endemic in work. Employees of all types are learning to cope with new technology, and many of them fear that the new technology will take their jobs. And adding to their fear of being replaced by a machine is their fear of the large numbers of foreign workers who have immigrated to most EC countries. Those foreigners provide not only a competitive pool of cheap labor but they also bring different cultures into traditional neighborhoods. Xenophobia is on the rise in many countries as a result. The opening of the frontiers to Eastern Europe will further exacerbate the situation.

General employment trends in the EC share many characteristics found in the United States. European employees, on average, are well trained, well paid, and work in the service sector. The education level of the work force has climbed throughout the postwar era. Today 26.6 percent of people are still in school at the age of nineteen compared to 18.8 percent in 1970 (CEC 1988c:10). European education frequently contains good vocational education programs which have improved the quality of the work force. In industry, 63 percent of the work force is classified as skilled. (Of the twelve member states, only the United Kingdom has over 50 percent of its industrial work force in unskilled jobs [CEC 1990j: 8].) Real wages have continued to climb since the 1950s, even though the rate of climb slowed after 1975 (CEC 1989k: 55). The better paid employees in the EC today have incomes close to those in the United States, even though the average remains below that in the United States. The economies in Europe have become increasingly dependent on the service sector as they have in the United States. The service sector supplies the most jobs (as it does in the United States), providing 58.8 percent of total employment. Almost all the new jobs added in the 1980s have been in the service sector. Industry provides jobs for 33.3 percent of the work force in the EC and agriculture 7.9 percent (CEC 1989p: 120). Jobs in these two sectors continued to decline during the 1980s. One other important trend in the EC is similar to one found in the United States: Women are entering the work force in increasing numbers; they comprise 38.7 percent of the work force (CEC 1989a: 114).

The EC has experienced a significant decline in labor-unit costs throughout the 1980s. If real unit-labor costs are set at 100 in 1980, they had fallen to 92.8 by 1989 (CEC 1988a: 38:42). The decline occurred because the annual rate of increase in wages was lower than that of productivity throughout the decade (CEC 1989k: 55). (Although the United States has a higher level of productivity, the EC annual rate of productivity growth is higher, so the gap between the two regions is quite narrow today.)

Four main problems are associated with employment in the EC at the present time: unemployment, regional differences, the changing nature of work, and the migrant work force. Each of the problems is a political issue which the governments of the member states of the EC have to address. Each is also now a problem which confronts the EC.

Unemployment is the most serious of the four problems. The problem has persisted since the first oil crisis in the 1970s. The economies in the EC have failed to create new jobs in adequate numbers to replace those lost in the economic restructuring which has occurred since that crisis. The failure has troubled labor specialists and public authorities throughout the EC and has produced mountains of research. Today, the unemployment average in the EC is 9.3 percent, down from the double digit figures of a few years ago but still unacceptably high. Three characteristics of unemployment add to its seriousness. One is that unemployment is twice as high among persons under 25 as those over 25. Many young people in the EC are maturing with no experience in the work place, creating an economic waste and a serious social problem. Another is that half of the unemployed are unemployed for at least one year (CEC 1989k: 113-120). As labor specialists know, the longer a person is unemployed, the more difficult it is for that person to return to the work force. The third is that the unemployed are not evenly distributed throughout the EC. They are concentrated in areas of general economic decline, frequently where the dominant industry has closed. New enterprises usually are not attracted to poor areas, and the unemployed have skills which are not needed in today's job market, so the outlook for the unemployed in those areas is grim.

Recent developments have added a new dimension to unemployment in the EC. One of the anticipated benefits of 1992 is job creation and, indeed, jobs are being created. About three million jobs are expected to be created in 1990 and 1991 and this increase includes both service and manufacturing jobs. However, unemployment probably will not decline as much as it did the previous two years because the labor force is expected to grow by two million in the two-year period for two reasons (CEC 1990b: 15). Economic recovery is bringing more women into the work force and the collapse of Eastern Europe is bringing a flood of working-age immigrants into Western Europe.

Regional differences, the second problem, are particularly significant in relation to unemployment, but other aspects of regional differences are important as well. Every average figure which is given to describe employment in the EC disguises wide variations among the member states. Wages, productivity, education, employment patterns, and levels of social protection vary widely. The addition of Greece, Spain, and Portugal in the 1980s exacerbated an already serious difference in income levels in the various regions. The ratio between income levels in the richest and poorest regions increased from 5 to 14 after the addition of the countries with their relatively lower levels of economic development (Molle & Cappellin 1988: 2).

The variations inhibit the formation of a common labor market. Europeans who live in chronically depressed regions with poor employment opportunities frequently lack the skills and the means to take jobs available in more prosperous regions. Many Europeans regard the differences as socially unjust and economically inefficient (Molle 1988: 71–73) and have little confidence in the corrective forces of a free market.

They expect political action from both national governments and the EC to alleviate regional differences.

The jobs which Europeans perform today differ dramatically from those which they performed ten years ago. While many of the changes are necessary for modernization, the social costs are high, and pressure is growing for political action to protect employees against the worst effects. The introduction of new technology puts constant pressure on the work force for flexibility and training. Employees worry about losing jobs and learning new skills. Employers worry about skill shortages and the cost of training. They fear battles with their employees when they want to introduce new technology. Old work rules may prevent the successful implementation of new technology. Labor unions attempt to protect their members by negotiating special agreements to govern the introduction of new technology. Many national governments have passed laws to facilitate the introduction of new technology. The problem of introducing new technology into the work place remains one of the most challenging in the EC today.

The growth of the black economy is another change in the work situation. The traditional black economy has long been a feature of work in certain sectors, such as tourism and construction. Employers hire workers to do low-skilled tasks without officially registering their employment in order to evade social security payments and costly labor regulations. The traditional black economy is estimated to contribute more than 10 percent of the GDP in Italy, Spain, Portugal, and Greece but probably it is an increasing part of the GDP in other countries of the EC as well (CEC 1989k: 131). Now the competitive pressures associated with the global economy appear to be exacerbating the situation. A growing number of manufacturers resort to subcontracting in order to contain costs. Subcontracting facilitates hiring black labor, and an open labor market will make it more difficult for national authorities to check on such illegal hiring. Another type of black economy also appears to be growing, and it involves highly paid, and therefore highly taxed, professionals. The unregulated exchange of services among professionals such as lawyers and accountants is assumed to be widespread in every country in the EC. National governments as well as the EC have so far not found ways to stop the growth of the black economy.

The third major problem relating to the changing world of work has to do with the growth of what is called in the EC "atypical work." Atypical work includes part-time work, temporary work, seasonal work, and work on fixed-term contracts. All forms of atypical work are growing. Forty percent of the jobs created between 1985 and 1988 are part-time. At the present time, fourteen million employees are engaged in part-time work and ten million in temporary jobs (CEC 1990k). Atypical work is considered to be essential in order to give firms needed flexibility; however, employees engaging in atypical work may not have the same protections as employees in standard work. In particular, concern is growing that some employers are using part-time work to avoid costly social costs, and many employees may be trapped in these jobs because full-time jobs are not available to them.

The fourth major problem regarding employment concerns the presence of large numbers of migrants in the work force of many countries in the EC. Most of the migrants come from countries to the south of the EC such as Turkey, Yugoslavia, and the countries of North Africa. They were invited in when Western Europe experienced labor shortages in the prosperous decades following World War II. They remained, married, and had children but did not integrate into the societies where they live. Today about eight million migrants live in the EC (CEC 1990a). Migrants have been the focus of social tension with some Europeans blaming them for high unemployment and social security costs (Miller 1981).

More recently, the EC has experienced an influx of persons from Eastern Europe and many persons fear that many more will come if jobs cannot be created in Eastern Europe. That fear can reach epic proportions when one considers that Eastern Europe has 93 million persons of working age and the Soviet Union has 185 million (CEC 1990b: 35). The EC, in an act of enlightened self-interest, has responded to the threat with numerous aid programs to encourage economic recovery.

## INTRODUCTION TO NATIONAL POLICIES

The "social dimension" of the 1992 initiative is designed to supplement national social policies which may be weakened by the formation of the internal market. National laws which protect working people appear to be most at risk; therefore, persons who want to understand the social dimension of the European Community should first become acquainted with the panorama of national policies which protect working people. They also need to understand the political situation in the member states at the time of the 1992 initiative.

The welfare state is a well-known characteristic of Western Europe. In the decades following World War II, Europeans became accustomed to a wide range of benefits and protections. Even Conservative governments did not eliminate the welfare state; they only sought to curtail its growth and to limit its constraint on private industry. The average percent of GDP spent on social protection among the nine member countries of the EC in 1980 ranged from 30.4 percent in The Netherlands to 19.8 percent in Italy (CEC 1989a: 135). The growth in social spending had outpaced the growth of GDP throughout the postwar era.

European employees expect the government to protect them from the hazards of work and to promote high standards in the work place. The legal rights of employees are deeply embedded in the European value system. They are endorsed by most important political parties and promoted by strong labor unions. Every national government in the European Community has a range of laws for employees which extends well beyond legal protections in the United States. Some of the laws originated in the last century and more were added in the reform era following World War II. The rights of employees were further extended in the late 1960s and early 1970s in response to militant demands from employee organizations. Today, European employees accept the idea that some rights may have to be limited, but they will resist any serious erosion of their rights.

Although all countries have extensive social policies, the actual body of law varies from country to country as a result of historical, economic, and cultural differences. For example, German employee laws are detailed and give workers extensive rights inside the work place and a wealth of social security provisions. The low-context German culture, the Nazi era, and postwar prosperity have all played a role in shaping the distinctive features of their employment laws. In contrast, British employee laws are less detailed and leave more to be determined by collective bargaining. Such latitude derives from the British culture in which tradition plays a strong role. Less detailed labor laws are also connected to the British common law tradition.

## SOCIAL POLICIES IN THE MEMBER STATES

The various national social policies can be divided into four categories: laws which apply directly to working conditions; laws which extend benefits to employees (comparable to fringe benefits in the United States); laws which affect industrial relations; and laws which provide rights to information about the work place and which establish rights to participate in making decisions affecting the work place. Each category will be examined in this chapter in order to give an overview of the current situation in the member states.

The term social policy is used interchangeably with employee policies in this chapter as they are commonly used in the EC. The interchange may cause some confusion when, later in the book, environmental policy is dealt with as a social policy. The environment at work is, however, an important part of environmental policy, so consideration of the topic is justified.

The unique aspect of European laws which apply to working conditions is the underlying assumption that work is a right which governments are responsible for protecting. The constitutions of a number of countries list the right to work among human rights; consequently, the hiring and firing rights of management are carefully circumscribed by law. An employee has the right to his job, which is defined in an individual employment contract. Employers who want to fire or lay off an employee must follow steps defined by law. Those steps generally include early notification, a written explanation, and severance pay. Employers may also be required by law to inform a workers' council and the local employment office before a layoff. Most governments have made it easier for employers to fire workers in recent years, but the protection is still extensive.

In other respects, national laws affecting working conditions resemble those in the United States. Laws regulate working hours, extend special protection to certain categories of employees, and usually set minimum wages. Sex discrimination is illegal in all EC countries. Laws for health and safety exist in all countries but vary considerably in degree and nature from the north to the south of Europe.

Important differences exist among national laws which apply to part-time or temporary work. Several countries require that part-time workers be given the same social protection as full-time employees. The United Kingdom, on the other hand, includes only permanent, full-time employees under the protection of employee laws. One-third of the work force is thus excluded, so any change in the law would significantly increase labor costs in the United Kingdom (CEC 1989d: 16). Not surprisingly, the United Kingdom has resisted efforts by the EC to harmonize labor legislation.

Vacations, maternity leave, and health insurance are all voluntary fringe benefits in the United States. They are determined by law in most EC states; moreover, Europeans regard such benefits as a right. As in the first category of employee laws, national variations are considerable. The resulting costs for employers also vary considerably and become a consideration for international firms planning new investments. Danish, Spanish, and French employees are all legally entitled to thirty days of paid annual leave. The Irish are entitled to three weeks. British employees have no legal entitlement to a paid holiday (CEC 1989u: 23). (British employees covered by collective agreements have twenty to twenty-seven vacation days.)

Training is another important item of employee benefits. Government and company expenditures on training are growing steadily. The French law on training is probably the most advanced in the EC. French firms employing more than ten persons must devote a minimum of 1.1 percent of their pay bill to training according to a 1976 law (CEC 1987b: 29). Since 1988, the French government also gives firms tax credits to encourage training programs.

Industrial relations systems vary greatly among the members of the EC. In general, however, the relationship among the government, labor unions, and employer associations is closer than it is in the United States. Corporatism is a characteristic common in many EC countries. Labor unions and employer associations frequently serve on government boards dealing with such issues as unemployment and social security. European governments frequently play a role in major wage settlements. In the past, income policies were common. Today, the government is more likely to bring informal pressure to bear on the negotiators for wage restraint. The government may designate the participants in collective bargaining, topics to be included in collective agreements, and the binding effect of agreements. In many countries, a peace obligation is enforced for the duration of a contract. Special labor courts exist in most countries to resolve legal questions arising in the industrial relations system.

The fourth category of employee laws deals with information and participation rights, an important and complex topic which will be discussed in Chapter 7. Such laws typically provide for the election of a workers' council by employees in firms above a certain size. The workers' council has rights to information about the firm and may have the right to be consulted on issues which affect jobs. Information and participation rights have been part of the legal system in most European countries for many years. Those rights were also one of the central issues in labor demands during the 1970s. Labor unions will fight any attempt to weaken national laws governing information and participation rights.

## THE POLITICS OF SOCIAL POLICY

In the 1980s, the political situation in the member states which had supported the growth of the welfare state changed. Chronic economic problems and budget deficits forced a reconsideration of values and priorities. The electorate shifted to the right. Social-democratic parties and labor unions, the traditional proponents of employee interests, found themselves on the defensive. Proponents of the interests of private business became more assertive. Conservative governments chipped away at the edges of the welfare state.

A profile of the situation in three major countries of the EC illustrates the general trend. The three countries are the United Kingdom, the Federal Republic of Germany, and France. The factors that will be noted are the significant political actors, the relevant laws and issues, and the general environment in the country.

The United Kingdom never fully recovered from World War II. Economic problems reached crisis proportions in the 1970s. The conventional wisdom blamed the British disease on an excessive welfare system and an archaic industrial relations system. In 1979, the Conservative government led by Margaret Thatcher was elected, in part, due to a sizable shift of votes in the working class away from the Labour party. The government limited social spending but did not eliminate traditional aspects of the welfare system such as the national health service. The government encouraged the growth of decentralized collective bargaining. Wages grew and continued to grow at the highest rate in the EC; however, unemployment grew as well in the early years of the Thatcher government.

British labor unions were at their weakest. The Labour party, their traditional defender, was torn apart by dissension. British labor unions lacked a strong, central authority to fight the hostility of the Thatcher government. The decline of the manufacturing sector led to large declines in union memberships. The government enacted laws to further limit labor union power. By 1988, British labor unions, always among the most nationalistic in the EC, were ready to reverse their historic opposition to the EC. They invited Jacques Delors, the President of the Commission, to address the annual conference of the Trade Union Congress and warmly greeted his announcement regarding the "social dimension" (Delors 1988).

British employee law more closely resembles the American than it does that of other EC states. Employees have relied on collective bargaining and common-law precedents more than on written protection. British managers have had more autonomy in hiring and firing than continental managers. Britain is almost unique in the EC in having no legislation for workers' councils. British workers were represented in the work place by traditionally strong shop stewards. A few laws have been enacted under requirements set by EC directives, such as the law of equal rights for women in the work place. Health and safety form one area where British law has generally been more advanced than on the continent.

The British economy appeared to be improving during the 1980s, so Thatcherism became the economic doctrine of the era. Economic liberalism and individual responsibility were two of the hallmarks of the doctrine. The British welfare state, which had never been as extensive as some on the continent, lost support. Only the growing demand for unemployment compensation kept the proportion of spending on social programs from declining as a percent of GDP.

The FRG also had a conservative government in the 1980s, but the Christian Democratic government of Helmut Kohl faced a less extreme crisis and followed more moderate policies. The ideological gap between the Social Democratic government of Schmidt and the Christian Democratic government of Kohl which followed it was not great. Both acted cautiously to assure that conditions were not only conducive to growth in the economy but also to social peace. German culture supports corporatism in which relevant interest groups participate in government decision making. It also promotes a social partnership between labor and management rather than the adversarial style common in Britain and the United States. Labor and management may not like each other any better in the FRG than they do in Britain, but the German culture forces at least the appearance of responsible behavior. The result is a rather steady evolution in policy making and in the formation of policies which have broad support.

One of the interesting differences between the Thatcher and Kohl governments is their responses to social policies in the EC. Margaret Thatcher has been vociferous in her opposition to the "social dimension." The Germans have been leaders in designing EC social policy. The reason for the differing positions of the two Conservative governments is the fact that the FRG has one of the most advanced sets of social policies in the EC. German firms pay high social costs and their competitive position will be enhanced if firms in other countries must meet similar standards. Furthermore, Germans across the political spectrum are proud of German codetermination, the policy which gives German employees extensive rights to participate in decision making in the work place. That policy could be weakened by the formation of the internal market. German firms could move beyond the reach of German law but still service the German market.

The organizational structure of German labor unions is as simple as the British is complex. Where Britain has over one hundred unions and no clear lines of jurisdiction, Germany has seventeen industrial unions all belonging to one umbrella organization. (Germany does have other unions, but with the exception of the white-collar union, they have little importance.) German labor unions are powerful, sophisticated, and rich compared to their British counterparts. They cultivate an image of responsibility and seldom evoke the hostility which sometimes falls on British unions. In the 1970s, German labor unions could demand and win reform of the codetermination laws. They also achieved significant wage increases for their members. In the 1980s, however, they had to moderate their demands in the face of the new political and economic climate. Their two targets became jobs and the defense of living standards.

The struggles against unemployment and in defense of living standards, which occupied German unions in the 1980s, occupied labor unions throughout the EC at that time. Labor unions were on the defensive against charges that their successes in the 1970s caused the problems of the 1980s. They were weakened by the loss of the traditional industrial base of labor union membership. They also confronted the growing power of employers and declining sympathy from the government. Throughout the EC, national labor unions, despite the moderation of their demands, were increasingly frustrated in their efforts to promote the interests of their members. The forces which compelled the British labor unions to a greater interest in the EC also compelled the more powerful German labor unions, as well as those of the other ten member states.

The German employee is one of the most coddled in the world. The law protects employees from job loss and gives them extensive social protections. They have status under a highly developed apprentice system which is sustained in law. In addition, German codetermination is probably unparalleled in the world for the legal authority it gives German employees in decision making. The German system of employee rights has developed slowly over many decades. It is associated with the German record of economic success. Many Germans, with new-found confidence, see it as a model for Europe.

France in the 1980s has experienced a lessening of the ideological divisions which have characterized it throughout its modern history. Its labor unions, however, are still divided among competing communists, socialists, and social democrats; consequently, French labor unions are weak, and the rate of membership is among the lowest in the EC. The ideological gap between labor and management remains wide as well. A social partnership is not in the French culture.

French employee law extends the usual protections found in Western Europe. It is particularly advanced in the protection of the families of employees and of women. The French participation rights exist more on paper than in practice. The Socialist government made significant reforms in the law when it first came to power in the 1980s, but more recently the recovery of the economy has become the priority and the reform effort has slowed. The leaders of the Socialist government know that improvements for French employees result in increased costs for French employers and a resulting loss in competitiveness; consequently, the French government supports efforts in the EC for the "social dimension." EC social policies will benefit French employees but not at the cost of French firms because firms throughout the EC will incur similar costs.

This brief look at three countries points out important reasons why pressure is growing for an expanded role for the EC in the formation of social policy:

1. Countries with the most advanced policies fear that firms will be able to take advantage of the internal market and move to countries with weaker policies. Such an advantage could set off a force against national social policies known as "social dumping."

2. Socialist governments which favor advances in social policy cannot enact such policies at the national level without harm to the competitive position of national firms; therefore, those governments favor a "level playing field"—a higher and more uniform level of social spending in the EC.

3. Labor unions and other groups who favor social policies frequently find that the prevailing ideology in their member state is inimical to them; therefore, they are looking increasingly to EC institutions for redress.

*Chapter 4*

---

# The Social Dimension: Its Relationship to the 1992 Initiative

In 1988, the Commission added a social dimension to the 1992 initiative (CEC 1988k). Work on the economic proposals contained in the White Paper on the Internal Market had been going on for three years before the Social Dimension was added. Inevitably, questions were raised about the necessity and the status of the new addition. The Commission claimed that social policy had always been implied by the 1992 initiative and that the social proposals were not secondary to the original economic proposals. Many business groups, as well as the British government, disputed the Commission's claims. For the first time, the 1992 initiative became the subject of serious public controversy.

The controversy over the Social Dimension is probably, in reality, the controversy over the future of European integration. Those who oppose the Social Dimension but support the original 1992 proposal see European integration in economic terms. For them, the role of the EC is to be the police officer who prevents national governments from interfering with the internal market. The market itself is to be free, operating under economic laws of the marketplace and with a minimum of regulations. Those who support the Social Dimension have a more qualified belief in the economic laws of the marketplace. They foresee a role for the EC in which it not only restrains national policies, but also supplements or replaces national policies, the effectiveness of which has been undermined by economic integration. The story of the Social Dimension—its history, extent, and justification—is a part of the story of the struggle to shape the future of European integration.

This chapter is divided into three parts in order to present the highlights of that story. The three parts are: the development of social policy in the EC before the proposal for a social dimension; the reasons for the Social Dimension; and a summary of the document.

## THE DEVELOPMENT OF SOCIAL POLICY BEFORE
## THE SOCIAL DIMENSION

The Treaty of Rome, which serves as the basis for EC law, has few provisions for social policy. The framers of the treaty expected social policy to remain the responsibility of national governments. The primary responsibility about employees, which the treaty gives to the EC, is to assure the free movement of labor as one of the four essential freedoms. (The other three are the free movement of goods, services, and capital, which, along with the right of establishment, lay the basis for the common market.) Articles 117 and 118 refer to the competence of member states in formulating social policy, but Article 118 contains the proviso that "the Commission shall have the task of promoting close cooperation between member states in the social field." Article 100 also empowers the Council of Ministers to act when divergent social policies harm competition. In both Article 100 and Article 118, the role of the EC is not to set a new EC social policy, but rather to draft a framework within which national governments would harmonize their own social policies.

The treaty gives the EC two specific tasks in regard to social policy. One is to prepare an annual report on social developments in the EC, and the other is to manage the Social Fund, which has become an important source for retraining workers harmed by technological change. The right of the EC to enact social policy may also be derived from three other provisions in the treaty. Subsection G of Article 54 empowers the EC to coordinate the measures which member states take in order to protect the interests of their citizens against harmful action by companies or firms. Article 119 gives the EC the responsibility to assure equal pay for men and women. Article 235 does not specifically address social policy but it does provide a wedge which the EC can use. That wedge is the implied power clause of the treaty, which allows the EC to take appropriate measures to attain the objectives of the treaty even though the treaty has not provided the necessary powers. The preamble of the treaty states that a purpose of the treaty is to provide for "the constant improvement of the living and working conditions of their people" and Article 2 states that one of the tasks of the EC is "an accelerated raising of the standard of living." Thus, the EC may claim responsibility for employees.

In the first decade of its existence, the EC did not seek to exercise authority over social policy, but it did enact a few measures to facilitate the free movement of workers. By the end of that decade, however, social unrest was widespread in Western Europe. Leaders of the EC at The Hague Summit in 1969 stated that they were ready to "enlarge, deepen and extend" their responsibilities. Many of those leaders were sympathetic to social issues and close to the labor unions in their countries; consequently, the EC considered a number of ambitious proposals for social policies and enacted several in the 1970s. The tone of the decade was set by the Social Action Program, which was accepted by the Council in 1974. That program provided the basis for wide-ranging action in social policy.

Industrial democracy was, perhaps, the topic which attracted the most attention in social policy during that decade. Throughout the 1970s, the EC labored over proposals to give employees legal rights inside their place of work. The two most famous proposals are the Fifth Directive and the European Company Statute. Both of those proposals are still under consideration, so they will be discussed more fully in Chapter 7. One should note, as evidence of the thinking in the EC during the 1970s, that neither was perceived as radical when they were proposed. They were designed to complement existing national laws and not to institute a new right. Both were drafted before the first enlargement of the EC. All governments among the six original members of the EC had laws requiring worker participation. Worker participation was called a "democratic imperative" in a paper on the Fifth Directive written by the Commission (CEC 1975b).

Another aspect of social policy in the 1970s grew out of the fear of employees regarding mounting unemployment, especially sudden or unnecessary job loss. They wanted to be informed by their employers about the financial status of their firm and about other developments which might affect employment. Labor unions demanded that both national governments and the EC enact laws to give employees extensive rights to information in the work place. The demand was so pervasive in the 1970s that one authority referred to it as a "disclosure bandwagon" (Peel 1979: 122). The EC responded to the pressure by enacting two directives in the 1970s on information and consultation rights. The 1975 directive on collective redundancies layoffs requires member states to enact laws directing companies considering reductions in their work forces to inform their employees and to consult with them (CEC 1975a).

It is the first EC legislation requiring firms also to prepare a study on ways to lessen the harmful effects of a proposed layoff. This provision is modeled on German law that requires a "social plan" before a layoff.

A 1977 directive requires firms to inform and consult with employees when a change of ownership takes place. It applies to acquisitions, mergers, and takeovers of businesses or parts of a business. If the change will affect the work force, the employer must consult the employees "in good time on such measures with a view to seeking agreement" (CEC 1975a).

Neither the 1975 nor the 1977 directive caused much controversy. Both were accepted within a few years of their proposal. They complemented existing national legislation and rested on values then broadly accepted. A similar passage was given to a directive accepted in 1980 which assures the protection of employees if an employer becomes insolvent (CEC 1980a). A very different response, however, awaited the famous Vredeling proposal in 1980. It proposed to require multinational corporations to inform and consult with their employees regularly. The Commission was surprised by the angry response from business because the Commission thought that the proposal was a logical extension of previous legislation. However, conditions were different by 1980, and the balance of power between employers and employees had shifted to the employers, with whom it remains.

The decade the 1970s was a productive period for other aspects of a broad social policy as well. The EC embarked on an ambitious program for women (see Chapter 6). It also expanded the Social Fund between 1972 and 1976. The Social Fund became the second largest item in the EC budget after agriculture. The Council approved an action program on health at work in 1974. The EC set up the Standing Committee on Employment and began regular consultations with labor unions through the Tripartite Committee on Labor, Government, and Management.

Three institutions were founded by the EC during the decade to carry on work relevant to employment. One, located in Dublin, is the European Foundation for the Improvement of Living and Working Conditions. Its purpose is to collect information and to encourage research on work humanization and new forms of work, a topic of great interest in Western Europe. Another is the European Center for the Development of Vocational Training (CEDEFOP) in Berlin, a fortuitous location because much of the Center's work will be on solving the enormous problems of vocational training in Eastern Europe. The third institution operates under the direction of European labor unions but is funded by the EC. It is the European Trade Union Institute in Brussels. It carries on a great deal of research on labor topics and publishes an annual report on collective bargaining in Western Europe.

The mid-1970s was probably the high tide of European social policy. By the end of the decade, social policy was out of favor in the member states and the EC itself was caught in a tide of sentiment against integration. When revitalization of the integration effort occurred in the 1980s, it was motivated by economic concerns, not by social ones.

## WHY THE SOCIAL DIMENSION

The two major documents which form the background to the Social Dimension are the Single European Act and the White Paper on the Internal Market. As discussed previously, the SEA sets the goal for the creation of the internal market by 1992 and amends Article 100 of the Treaty of Rome so that laws necessary for the internal market can be enacted by a qualified majority vote in the Council. According to the SEA, laws providing for the free movement of persons or laws dealing with the rights and interests of employed persons continue to require unanimous consent in the Council. The importance of the requirement for unanimity cannot be overemphasized. The requirement relegates most proposals on social policy to the slow track of EC policy making. It forms the basis for the current battle between proponents of social policy in the Commission and the Parliament and opponents led by Margaret Thatcher.

The SEA makes only two changes to the provisions on social policy first set down in the Treaty of Rome. One change concerns health and safety, which are given a unique status in social policy. Health and safety proposals, alone among social proposals, may be enacted by a qualified majority in the Council, and the EC has made remarkable progress on those proposals in the last few years. The other change concerns the responsibility of the Commission to develop a dialogue between labor and management at the European level. The goal of the dialogue would be to reach a common position on European employee issues. This rather ambiguous provision may some day provide the basis for European collective bargaining. (At the present time, most employer associations strongly oppose this possibility of collective bargaining at the EC level.)

The SEA contains two other passages which are relevant for social policy. The preamble states that members have a commitment "to improve the economic and social situation by extending common policies and pursuing new objectives." Title V concerns the need for economic and social cohesion. It primarily deals with regional disparities, and it merges the Social Fund with regional and agricultural funds to form the Structural Fund.

While the SEA constitutes a major step toward economic integration, it adds only a tentative half step toward a European social policy. The other document dealing with the single market, the White Paper, does not even deal with social policy. It is an economic document cast in the philosophy of economic liberalism. The purpose of the document is to set out the policies necessary to eliminate barriers to the free movement of the factors of production, so it deals with employee issues only insofar as they concern the free movement of workers and professionals.

Directives are proposed to remove the remaining restrictions. For example, giving residence permits for citizens of an EC country who want to work in another EC country. The different standards for vocational education are targeted for harmonization. The document also contains proposals for the mutual recognition of university degrees and the accreditation of professionals. In each case, the White Paper proposes to eliminate national policies which limit market access. The focus is on the formation of the single market and not on possible dislocations arising from that formation. The need for a discussion on social issues and the structural funds is briefly mentioned, but it is the only exception in this essentially economic document.

A key question related to the topic of this chapter is whether the neglect of social policy in the White Paper is only a matter of priorities. One possible answer is that the Commission started the revitalization of the EC with an economic program first simply because it was expedient to do so. If expedience is the answer, then social policy is not relegated to a second-class order of policies. Rather it forms, with economic policy, an equal part of the whole integration process. The other possible answer is that the EC, in accepting the White Paper, accepted the assumptions that economic liberalism would in itself provide the corrections for short-term social dislocations, so the EC need not and should not formulate a social policy which is equal to the policy of the single market. The British government and those associated with the Bruge group believe that the latter answer is correct. They oppose EC social policy not on a case-by-case basis but rather on the grounds that EC social policy in itself undermines the very basis for success of the 1992 initiative. The Commission appears to accept the first answer. The following quotation from the White Paper seems to support the Commission's acceptance as well: "As far as social aspects are concerned, the Commission will pursue the dialogue with governments and social partners to ensure that the opportunities afforded by completion of the Internal Market will be accompanied by appropriate measures aimed at fulfilling the Community's employment and social security objectives" (CEC 1985b: 8).

Although the Social Dimension was not added to the single market policy until 1988, discussions about the social implications of the single market began among several groups almost simultaneously with the drafting of the White Paper. Jacques Delors convened a meeting in 1985 of the social partners, which became institutionalized as the Val Duchese process. That process led to the establishment of a number of working groups to study different aspects of the problems of employment and the introduction of new technologies. The European Parliament approved a report in 1986 which urged the Commission to prepare a plan setting out the necessary measures for establishing a European social area so that economic and social progress could proceed in tandem (CEC 1988c). (The idea of a European social area had been proposed by the French as early as 1981.) Belgium proposed an EC platform of basic social rights when it held the presidency of the Council in 1987. The Commission organized twelve seminars to consider different social aspects of the internal market between 1987 and 1988 (CEC 1989n). Then the Commission appointed an interdepartmental working party whose report paved the way for the Social Dimension (CEC 1988j). The final okay for a social policy came from the Council at the Hanover Summit in June 1988. The final communiqué states, "The European Council stresses the importance of the social aspects of progress toward the 1992 objectives" (CEC 1988h: Annex).

## THE JUSTIFICATION FOR THE SOCIAL DIMENSION

Those who argue for a social dimension point to two basic reasons why social policies will be necessary. One is that the free movement of workers, an essential component of the internal market, cannot exist unless the EC acts to create the conditions necessary for it to operate. The second reason is that the process of creating the internal market will have some negative social consequences. The EC should anticipate those consequences and, if possible, alleviate them in order to attain the social cohesion called for in the Single European Act.

The members of the interdepartmental working party of the Commission concentrated much of their study on the topic of the free movement of labor in the EC. They learned that many previous assumptions about labor mobility were no longer valid. They rejected the argument that labor mobility would provide a solution for unemployment among unskilled workers. They found that the new migrants were skilled employees. They also found that firms faced shortages of skilled employees, so they concluded that a flexible and free labor market needed more uniform standards for job qualifications and better information on the availability of employment throughout the EC. They suggested that the EC act to propose policies 1) to harmonize national standards for vocational training, 2) to facilitate information about employment opportunities and living conditions in different countries, and 3) to assist in training employees for the new labor market (CEC 1988m: 20-30).

With the formation of the internal market, EC firms will restructure in order to locate in the most economic areas. They will also be able to streamline their operations, closing facilities made redundant by the single market. They will invest in new technologies. Such changes have social as well as economic consequences. Jobs will be lost or relocated and new skills will be required. The new job market will extend beyond the reach of national employee laws. The social consequences will bring about pressure for a social dimension to be added to the 1992 initiative.

Because unemployment has long been a serious problem in the EC, any trend which exacerbates unemployment, even over the short term, has serious political consequences. Although the internal market is predicted to increase employment by 1.8 million new jobs, certain categories of jobs will be lost and some regions will lose jobs (Cecchini 1988: 97). The Commission had studies made to identify sectors where the most changes could be anticipated when national barriers were removed. Those studies showed that the effect of the internal market on employment would not be uniform across all sectors. Certain jobs, such as those in the boilermaking industry, would be at high risk. All sectors which are suppliers to public administrations and state-owned firms would also be at high risk. Overall, fifty percent of industrial jobs would be vulnerable (CEC 1988m: 39-46). The jobs that will be created are expected to require skills different from the ones found among the workers being displaced, so the EC needs to be concerned about the cost and quality of training.

One of the major fears is that the creation of the internal market will increase regional disparities. Jobs will be lost in the periphery of the EC and gained in the rich core. In 1985, unemployment rates already were unacceptably high in certain periphery countries, such as Ireland, where 18.5 percent of the work force was unemployed (CEC 1989a: 126). Regional disparities have been increasing in the EC since 1973, and they pose a threat to integration. The Commission is not optimistic that the creation of the internal market in itself will ameliorate the situation.

According to one important report, "There is abundant evidence that those embarking upon the course of economic integration should not rely on simple beliefs about the benevolence of 'invisible hands'" (Padoa-Schioppa 1987: 21). According to the author's reasoning, the EC must intervene to assure that unemployment does not increase in the poorer regions of the EC.

The fear of social dumping is the most famous argument for a social dimension. The concept refers specifically to the possibility that firms will take advantage of the single market to relocate to countries in the EC where the level of legal protection for workers is lower. The relocating will bring downward pressure to bear on social conditions and so block social progress. Governments with a high level of social protection for workers, as well as labor unions, fear the negative consequences of the 1992 initiative. Some authorities refute the arguments, but the working party concluded that "the risk of social dumping exists and cannot therefore be discounted" (CEC 1988m: 66). The EC should harmonize national employee protections or establish uniform EC policies in order to assure that social dumping does not take place in the internal market.

## ANALYSIS OF THE SOCIAL DIMENSION OF THE INTERNAL MARKET

By 1988, progress on the 1992 initiative had reached the stage where it was deemed irreversible. Meanwhile the arguments in support of a social dimension accumulated, and the political pressure for it grew as well. The Commissioners became convinced that they needed to assure the public that individuals would not be harmed under the steamroller of the 1992 initiative. In the spring of 1988, Jacques Delors traveled to the annual conference of the European Trade Union Confederation in order to announce that a social dimension would be added to the 1992 initiative. During the course of the year, he traveled to many other labor union conferences with the same message. He told the British Trade Union Congress, "It would be unacceptable for Europe to become a source of social regression, while we are trying to rediscover together the road to prosperity and employment" (Delors 1988).

On September 14, 1988, the Commission issued the working paper *Social Dimension of the Internal Market* (CEC 1988k). The purpose of the document is to present a discussion of the social concerns raised by the creation of the internal market and of possible solutions to problems which may occur. The format of the document is similar to the White

Paper on Completing the Internal Market. The body of the paper contains a justification for the proposal as well as a discussion of the scope and objectives of the proposal. The EC is justified in making the proposal because, "the very process of consolidating the internal market may entail costs which, while likely to be very limited in time and space, may be considerable. It is essential to take account of these costs and alleviate them for reasons of equity and also to ensure the success of the process of strengthening the Community" (p. 2). The scope of the policy is limited to social problems arising from or exacerbated by the creation of the internal market. The responsibility for implementing the policy rests with both national authorities and the EC.

Annex II of the document lists the individual policies which will be proposed. It differs from the annex of the White Paper in that a schedule is not given for formulating the policies. Also, far fewer policies are proposed in this document compared to the annex of the White Paper, approximately 80 and 279, respectively.

The paper is a politically sensitive document. It is drafted in such a way as to appeal to employees without arousing opposition among employers. It contains some proposals which labor unions have sought for many years. On the other hand, the language of the paper is cautious. Respect is paid to the assumptions of economic liberalism. It states in the foreword that economic growth will "improve working conditions, employment prospects and, in short, the standard of living of Europeans in general." The foreword also contains the following important sentence: "It (the Social Dimension) is not in opposition to nor must it slow down the completion of the internal market." The statements in the foreword are countered in the body of the paper by an admission that the market may have detrimental social consequences which will require a social policy.

The paper maintains a careful balance between the sensitivities of national sovereignty and the recognition that some harmonization of national policies will be necessary. That balance has become the famous principle of *subsidiarity* that states that policies should always be made at the lowest possible level of government and that the EC should legislate only in areas where uniformity is absolutely necessary. The framers of the document reiterated the continued responsibility of national governments and their citizens for the protection of employees. "Not only are the benefits of greater harmonization of regulations debatable, except in the cases mentioned, but also a number of serious *difficulties* stand in the way of attaining it" (p. 27). Citizens can also protect themselves from many problems which may arise through normal, democratic processes in their own member state, so, *"fears of 'social dumping' are totally unfounded"* (p. 26).

Unemployment is the main target of concern in the document. Economic growth resulting from the creation of the internal market will alleviate the problem in the long run, but the EC needs to take measures to assure the free movement of labor and to assist certain categories of persons who will be most affected by the changes associated with growth. The arguments and proposals on the topic of unemployment reflect the earlier report of the interdepartmental working party. As in the earlier report, the document assigns an important role to the EC in the field of training in order to assure a mobile work force and to assist the unemployed.

One of the most important provisions in the document is almost lost amid the general denial of the need for EC policies to harmonize national employee policies: That the EC guarantee certain minimum health and safety standards. The subject is only briefly mentioned, but notice is given of the fact that measures dealing with health and safety require only a qualified majority vote in the Council. Health and safety is dealt with again in the conclusion of the document. That latter passage almost constitutes a reversal of the earlier homage paid to the beneficial effects of a free market: "The rules relating to the health protection and safety of workers at the work place will also have to be reinforced to prevent the freedom of movement of goods and services evolving under circumstances which would lead to a deterioration in living and working conditions" (p. 60).

In summary, the text of the document is by no means revolutionary. It proposes no sweeping transfer of power to the EC. Rather it deeply bows to the importance of national policies. It sets forth no grand design for EC social policies. Rather it pays respect to the curative powers of a free market. It does, very cautiously and almost ambiguously, refer to some areas where EC policy will be needed. Two of the most controversial areas, a European company law and a European charter of social rights, were briefly mentioned at the end of the document, but even a brief mention sufficed to alert those who fear an interventionist EC. Both issues have since led to major political confrontations in the EC.

Most of the proposals listed in the annex are not controversial. About eighteen of them deal with measures to eliminate barriers to the free movement of labor. Another sixteen deal with health and safety, and eleven with education and training, all topics with broad support. At least six proposals are only for studies or consultations. Several measures are of minor relevance, such as a recommendation for sharing family and work responsibilities, and a proposal for a senior-citizen pass.

Only four of the measures are highly controversial. Three of them were proposed many years ago but have been blocked in the Council. One deals with protection for part-time employees. The other two deal with issues relating to industrial democracy: a proposal for a directive to require international corporations to inform and consult with their employees and a proposal for a European company law. The fourth and only new proposal which is controversial is for a European charter of social rights. (Such a charter already exists in the Council of Europe.)

## CONCLUSION

The social policy of the EC has evolved through a number of stages since the first minor steps to achieve a free market for labor. The most active period was in the 1970s. In the 1980s, economic concerns took priority and led to the 1992 initiative. The rapid implementation of the internal market in turn led to renewed interest in social policy. Many feared that the changes associated with the consolidation of the internal market would result in a regression of standards for employees. The Commission responded to the fear by issuing the working paper *Social Dimension of the Internal Market* (CEC 1988k), in which areas of concern are noted, remedies proposed, and responsibilities shared between national authorities and the EC.

The Social Dimension is important because it constitutes recognition by the Commission that social problems will arise as a result of the creation of the internal market and that the Commission will undertake an activist policy to ameliorate the problems when necessary. The policy does not expand the role of the EC to social policy beyond the scope set in the 1970s. The policy is important not because it gives the EC new authority, but because it raises social concerns to an equal plane with the economic concerns. With the proclamation of the Social Dimension, the development of the 1992 initiative entered a new and highly controversial stage. The Social Dimension transformed a policy that had been primarily directed toward the elimination of national policies which obstructed a single market in the EC. The role of the EC was to preside over the elimination process. With the Social Dimension, the EC took on a more activist role. The benefits of the creation of the internal market were questioned.

Each of the proposals contained in the annex of the Social Dimension document must be submitted to the decision-making process of the EC.

Many will be proposed as directives which must be considered by the Parliament and accepted unanimously by the Council. A few privileged proposals will go forward by the same channels but with only the requirement of a qualified majority vote in the Council. The fate of the proposals, or at least the most important ones, will be important for employees in the EC. It will also be important in determining the nature of European integration in the next decades.

# Chapter 5

# The Politics of the Social Dimension

The Social Dimension marks an advance in European integration. It ties EC policies directly to the interests and values of the citizens of the member states. It was formed by European political processes—as distinct from a process that is the sum of politics in the twelve member states. It is also the stimulus for the continuing development of European politics. The validity of these assumptions will be discussed in this chapter using the concepts developed by functionalists in the early years of scholarly writing on the EC.

Theoretical literature on the EC thrived until the 1970s but declined in the years that followed. Only a few scholars, such as Juliet Lodge and Paul Taylor, kept the tradition alive during the years of Europessimism. The recent rash of writing on the EC marks the opening of a new era of EC scholarship which, so far, is largely descriptive and directed to a business audience.

A basic assumption which motivated the founders of the EC is that European integration is a goal worth seeking but one that should be constructed incrementally. According to this school of thought, the EC should undertake limited tasks for which it has been assigned limited amounts of sovereign power. The number of tasks or functions should gradually increase until the EC reaches a stage where it takes on the full range of attributes of a political system: processing demands, allocating values, and commanding legitimacy.

Ernst Haas, one of the most respected authorities in the early period of EC scholarship, defined integration as a process in which actors in the member states transferred their focus and loyalty from the member states to the EC, which had obtained authority over the member states (Haas 1966: 94). Haas also foresaw that the EC, in the pursuit of its assigned functions, would inevitably undertake additional, related tasks and thereby increase its scope of authority. This is called a spillover effect (Haas 1964).

Theorists who followed the work of Haas have been called *functionalists* or neofunctionalists. A uniform definition of the concepts does not exist. (See for example Taylor 1983 and Mutimer 1989.) However, the term *functionalist* will be used in the present discussion and the framework is based primarily on the work by James Caporaso (1974). Some of the key ideas or assumptions included in the following are:

1. Integration should be studied as a process and not as a final objective.
2. Integration involves the growing attachment between citizens in different countries and the EC.
3. The EC must be perceived as fulfilling needs or expectations of citizens that are not being satisfied at the national level.
4. The EC must have an effective policy-making process if it is to meet the demands of the citizens.
5. Economic integration and political integration are linked.

Functionalist theory involves the use of concepts familiar in political science. Interest articulation refers to the process by which the wants of citizens are expressed to political actors. Interest groups are the obvious mechanisms for interest articulation. Interest aggregation refers to the process by which different interests are brought together and merged into a demand that may be processed in the political system. Political parties frequently function to aggregate interests. Political systems have channels for processing demands and for converting them into outputs or policies that respond to citizen demands.

Persons who study the EC have been interested to discern if the EC is taking on the attributes of a political system with the ability to convert demands into outputs or policies through its own autonomous structures and responding to European political actors. James Caporaso distinguished a number of questions that need to be addressed in order to discern how the process of integration is proceeding (Caporaso 1974: 8). These questions can be restated as five questions which are particularly relevant to the discussion of the social dimension and its impact on European integration. They are:

1. Do European interest groups act at the EC level to articulate demands?
2. Do European elites act through the EC rather than through national channels?
3. Does an effective and autonomous EC bureaucracy exist?
4. Does the EC effectively communicate with Europeans?
5. Has the EC developed structures to perform binding political functions of policy making, implementation, and adjudication?

Each of these questions will be discussed in relation to the politics of the social dimension. The chapters that follow also contain information regarding the politics involved in making specific social policies. The picture that emerges is not a bold one of European politics at work, but rather a more subdued one in which the tentative outline of European politics is taking shape.

## DO EUROPEAN INTEREST GROUPS ACT TO ARTICULATE DEMANDS?

According to functionalist theory, interest groups should play an important role in the process of European integration to link the people to the EC and to assist in the democratic formulation of EC policy by articulation. A mutual dependence exists between the development of EC policies and EC interest groups. The EC must have policies that call into being EC interest groups that differ from national interest groups which act occasionally at the EC level. Such policies must be perceived by people in the member states as important for them. It is the role of the interest group both to communicate to the EC the types of policies desired by the people and to communicate to the people the relevance of the EC for them.

Policy making in the EC offers a number of points where interest groups can be active. The Commission has a constant need for information that interest groups may provide. The Commission regularly consults relevant interest groups when preparing a policy. Eurocrats working in the specialized directorate generals (DGs) frequently have much in common with interest group representatives. The Commission relies on specialized groups of experts for assessments of policies and members of the groups may be drawn from interest groups. The Parliament also offers a fertile ground for interest group activity. Certain political parties have well-developed ties with interest groups. The Parliament, as an institution, has assumed the mantle of champion of the peoples of Europe which draws it close to interest groups active in such areas as consumer rights or environmental concerns. The Council also is accessible to interest groups but probably has more frequent contacts with national interest groups than ones formed at the EC level. The Economic and Social Committee is less significant in the EC hierarchy than the three previously mentioned institutions, but it does provide a legitimate place for persons from interest groups inside the institutional framework of the EC.

The number of interest groups active in the EC has grown to exceed five hundred. In addition, lobbying activity is conducted by representatives of individual firms and also by representatives of national groups. Most of the EC interest groups are little more than a loose confederation of national interests and many are weak and underfunded organizations. However, three interest groups are noted for being well organized and influential. Two of them are actors in the area of the social dimension. They are UNICE (Union of Industries of the EC) and the ETUC (European Trade Union Confederation). (The third is COPA, which is the powerful agriculture lobby.) Both of these groups started as weak organizations representing diverse national groups from EC countries as well as other European countries.

UNICE was formed in 1958. Its members are national confederations of employers' associations in Western Europe. Its members generally play an influential role in the member states where they act as lobbies, but also serve on government boards and may participate in collective bargaining. UNICE is not a very large or very visible organization and avoids the public relations role sometimes played by American groups representing business. It serves primarily to provide the business viewpoint to institutions of the EC.

UNICE operated in a congenial atmosphere in Brussels until the EC began to consider social policies in the 1970s. At first, UNICE did not oppose the growth of EC authority in the social area, but later it moved to a more hostile posture. UNICE was and is opposed to any effort by the EC to establish a uniform requirement on worker participation. When the EC started to draft one of its first proposals containing a provision for worker participation, the Fifth Directive, UNICE did not reject the efforts. Indeed, it stated that proper worker participation could be constructive for firms (UNICE 1976). However, when the Commission issued the Vredeling proposal in 1980 to require multinational firms to inform and consult employees, UNICE engaged in a most vigorous campaign to defeat the proposal. A UNICE press release stated, "European employers said they could find no basis on practical or legal grounds for the proposal" (UNICE 1981).

UNICE officials took their case to the Council where they found support and the proposal was blocked. Their strategy was effective because their goal was to defeat the proposal and not to change it. Therefore, the Council offered the best opportunity. It only took the opposition or threat of opposition from one member state in order to block a proposal in the Council and UNICE could depend on the support of the British government. UNICE paid a price for its unbending opposition with both the Commission and the Parliament because support for social policies was strong in both of these institutions. Some persons in the Commission dismissed UNICE for what they deemed to be its negative posture. Even persons in the Directorate General for Industry, who would seem to be the natural allies of UNICE, were disturbed by the uncompromising opposition of UNICE toward worker participation.

When the EC launched the 1992 initiative, UNICE took on a new importance for European businesses. 1992 makes the EC the focal point for large businesses. Business people have important interests at stake in shaping the laws dealing with the creation of the internal market. One British business publication went so far as to state that employer associations are convinced that the days of national lobbying are ended (Institute of Personnel Management 1988). In this new atmosphere, UNICE has changed its tactics to be more proactive. In particular, it needs a constructive relationship with the Commission so that it can play a role in the important formative stages of 1992 policies. It is no longer enough to be able to block legislation in the Council by the support of one or two sympathetic governments. UNICE members want positive legislation from the EC in order to remove national barriers to business.

The Single European Act also compels UNICE, as well as other EC interest groups, to take a broader or more "European" position. Because a veto may no longer be cast in the Council on matters dealing with the internal market, UNICE must seek a wider coalition of support on such matters. In political science jargon, UNICE must aggregate the interests of its national members in order to appear to be articulating a European interest. Thus, when the EC widened its scope of activity with the 1992 initiative and reformed its policy-making process, it caused changes in the activity of UNICE which follow the lines foreseen by functionalist theorists.

When the Commission issued the Social Dimension, UNICE agreed that the EC should add a social dimension to the internal market. UNICE supports the harmonization of health and safety standards, and acknowledges the usefulness of a social dialogue with the EC and the ETUC. However, UNICE opposes EC efforts to force uniformity on member countries regarding worker participation. It also invokes frequent reference to subsidiarity, by which it means that the responsibility for social policies should remain primarily at the national level (UNICE 1988a).

UNICE apparently sees the acceptance of social dialogue as a small price to pay for a rapprochement with the Commission in order to participate in the formative stages of EC legislation. According to a British report, UNICE "views the Social Dialogue as an important forum in which the two sides of industry and the Commission together review developments and steps still to be taken to realise the internal market, and discuss social problems in their economic context" (Gill 1990: 34–35).

UNICE has sustained its moderate position even though the Commission has moved ahead in developing the Social Dimension. The Secretary-General of UNICE wrote a careful comment on the proposed charter of employee rights. (As discussed later, the Social Charter aroused the most controversy of the various social proposals in discussion in 1989.) He wrote, "UNICE has always been in favour of recognizing fundamental social rights" (Tyszkiewicz 1989: 24). He added, however, that social policy must not undermine the competitive position of European firms. As long as social policies do not threaten the competitiveness of EC firms, UNICE is prepared to play a constructive role in shaping EC social policy.

This brief history of UNICE shows an interesting dynamic at work. UNICE has shifted from a strategy of outright opposition to a bargaining strategy in response to two key developments. UNICE has a mandate from its members to further the completion of the internal market. It needs a working relationship with the Commission in order to achieve this goal. The second is the institutional changes resulting from the SEA. Even when the only goal of an interest group is to prevent the acceptance of a proposal, it can no longer rely on a strategy of seeking only one ally among the member governments in the Council in regard to the completion of the internal market.

The ETUC is the labor union counterpart of UNICE. It was formed primarily to provide direct contact with the EC for national labor confederations. Membership is open to any European, democratic labor confederation including ones from non-EC countries such as Sweden.

Unlike many international labor unions, the ETUC accepts members from diverse ideological positions as long as they are deemed to be democratic. For example, the separate Italian Catholic, communist, and social democratic labor federations are all members. This broad membership base gives the ETUC a strong position as the legitimate representative of European employees. On the other hand, it also has hampered the organization in lobbying on certain issues, such as worker participation, where the views of its members are divided.

Through the years, the ETUC has operated much as any interest group would in a national setting. Its officials have sought to develop rapport with significant persons in the EC and to gain access to EC institutions. Their success has varied from an intimate relationship with the Economic and Social Committee, where a large number of members are also members of a labor union, to a distant one with the Council which has been dominated by center-right governments throughout the 1980s. Parliament, under the control of its two largest parties—the Socialists and the Christian Democrat—supports many of the causes of the ETUC. The Commission has been the focus of much of the effort of the ETUC. ETUC officials have regular contacts with the civil servants in the relevant DGs. They usually have also been able to depend on a sympathetic hearing from the commissioner responsible for social policy. The portfolio for employment policy customarily goes to a commissioner from the center-left in European politics. This is the case at the present time when the relevant commissioner is Vasso Papandreou from the Greek Socialist party.

The officials of the ETUC have worked to project an image of the organization as a European pressure group that is reasonable and moderate and have avoided abrasive, confrontational tactics. Their style of operation and public relations is very similar to that of their northern members such as the Swedish and German labor confederations. Conferences are held, press releases are issued, reports prepared—all with the purpose of educating a supportive public opinion. Flamboyant acts such as a threat of a European strike do not appear to be in their file of tactics. Their visibility probably is not very high among Europeans.

The moderate stance of the ETUC is a strategy and does not arise out of a general acceptance of the status quo. Its ideology accords with democratic socialist values that are generally accepted throughout Western Europe. It espouses typical labor issues such as unemployment, but it also endorses broader social issues such as the environment and women's rights.

A study of the ETUC position on worker participation proposals in the EC reveals the difficulties that the group has in defining a common position among its diverse membership. The first proposals in the EC for worker participation were based on the German codetermination model which provides for a uniform structure of participation based on law. The initial ETUC response was ambiguous and remained so until the Commission issued the Vredeling proposal. The ETUC did not endorse either the European Company Statute or the Fifth Directive, the two proposals for worker participation which preceded the Vredeling proposal. Throughout the 1970s, the ETUC made only vague references of support for the principle of industrial democracy. The following quote indicates the ambiguity. "The objective of the trade union fight for economic democracy is not codetermination, worker control, asset formation, or any other such model" (ETUC 1983: 16).

In contrast, the ETUC fully endorsed the later proposal for worker participation known as the Vredeling proposal and fought for its acceptance. The explanation for the change is simple. No one structure of worker participation is acceptable to all the members of the ETUC. Practices and philosophies of participation are too diverse among the member countries. Therefore, the ETUC could not articulate support for the first proposals which were modeled too closely on the practice of codetermination. The Vredeling proposal differed from the earlier proposals in that it did not require the institutionalization of worker participation and therefore did not threaten existing norms among the members. It only supplemented national laws already in existence which required firms to disclose relevant information to their employees. Members of the ETUC knew that national laws on disclosure were inadequate to force .compliance on multinational corporations. Therefore, they were willing to join in support of an EC policy. The ETUC fought hard for the Vredeling proposal and had support from the Commission and the Parliament, but could not overcome opposition in the Council where UNICE was successful.

The ETUC supports the 1992 initiative. The support is somewhat surprising until one considers the situation in the member countries in the 1980s. National labor unions had not been able to prevent government austerity programs that affected employees. Neither had they been able to stem the growth of unemployment with its detrimental impact on union membership. Relations between governments and labor unions were strained both in countries with right-wing and left-wing parties in control. Spanish and French socialists put into effect austerity measures just as right-wing coalitions did in other countries. National labor unions turned to the EC in frustration with their failures at the national level. The most dramatic switch was made by the British Trade Union Congress, which had long been suspicious of any development across the Channel. The 1992 initiative promised economic revitalization and an increase in employment. The ETUC endorsed the initiative with uniform support from its members.

The ETUC was in a strong position to suggest to the commissioners that the economic measures contained in the 1992 initiative be supplemented by social ones. ETUC officials raised questions regarding the impact of 1992 on employees. The commissioners wanted public support for 1992 and the ETUC could supply it; consequently, they were receptive to the concerns of the ETUC. The result is the Social Dimension. The chain of circumstances leading from the 1992 initiative to the Social Dimension is clear evidence of the validity of functionalist assumptions regarding the forces bringing about European integration. A new economic policy spurred EC political activity which, in turn, led to a spillover into new social policy. The Commission has used the Social Dimension to mobilize support among employees throughout the EC. For their part, employees have turned to the EC when national channels of influence were blocked. Now the Social Dimension promises the enlargement of the scope of social policies in the EC and further encourages support for the EC and strengthens the ETUC. Additional developments will depend on how well the Commission is able to carry out the conversion function of transforming promises into outputs which have a direct impact on employees in the EC.

## ARE EUROPEAN ELITES ACTING THROUGH THE EC?

The answer to the second question is much briefer than the answer to the first one. European elites are acting through the EC today much more commonly than in the past because national governments do not appear to have the solutions to the major problems of economic growth and prosperity. As noted above, both business and labor leaders have turned to the EC to meet their demands. For different reasons, both have found national strategies inadequate. Evidence exists that national political leaders are also turning to the EC because they too find that national action is not adequate.

Political elites, acting in the Council and the Parliament, have accepted the rapid passage of measures to complete the internal market. Many of these measures remove the right of elites to enact separate national policies. Many eliminate cherished national prerogatives, such as the traditional Italian control on currency movements, in the pursuit of EC policies. Political elites accepted 1992 because national economic policies were not working. The economic recovery that coincided with (or resulted from) the implementation of the 1992 measures reinforced their commitment to the EC.

The success of 1992 has also made it good politics for leaders to identify with the EC. Most strive to appear to be good Europeans. They use the occasions of European summits in order to demonstrate to their constituencies that they are effective on the European stage. The failure of Margaret Thatcher to align herself as a part of the team of European elites was probably an important factor in her fall from power.

The willingness of political elites to work through the EC for economic policies is not necessarily matched with an equal regard for EC social initiatives. They could accept the Social Dimension as a general statement of social concern without necessarily signaling that they now regard the EC as the locus for social policies. Political leaders are moving cautiously and acting only when they see that the creation of the internal market is undermining the effectiveness of national social policies. They harmonize national policies in order not to place their country at a competitive disadvantage due to more stringent social laws. In addition, national political elites can still rely on the veto in the Council for social proposals which they oppose. They are not forced to strike a bargain with other national elites, as they must with economic policy.

One group of political elites where a significant shift of focus seems to have occurred is among leading socialist politicians. They appear to regard the EC as the most promising arena for the development of programs that they endorse. The role of Jacques Delors, a former cabinet minister in the French Socialist government, is well known but others have also been important to the development of the social dimension. Felipe Gonzalez used the occasion of the Spanish Presidency of the Council in order to promote EC social policies. Neil Kinnock has been instrumental in turning the British Labour party in a more European direction. The pattern continues throughout the EC (Dankert and Kooyman 1989). Today a convergence is found among the views of different socialist leaders, in contrast to the situation of the past when many were suspicious of the EC.

The answer to the question as to when and why European elites act through the EC rather than through national channels is that elites turn to the EC when national channels are blocked or ineffective for their objectives. The EC has become the accepted stage for economic policies and that, in turn, is leading to a spillover effect in regard to social policy. Elite behavior is adjusting accordingly.

## IS THE EC BUREAUCRACY EFFECTIVE AND AUTONOMOUS?

The third question concerns the autonomy and effectiveness of the EC bureaucracy. No one can study the evolution of social policy in the EC without being struck by the important role played by the bureaucracy. Two primary factors need to be recognized. Civil servants of the EC make a career commitment to the EC. They spend their work life in an EC milieu as distinct from actors in a national setting. The EC now has a cadre of civil servants who are approaching retirement after spending almost their entire working life inside the EC bureaucracy. In addition, EC civil servants work in specialized divisions or directorate generals in the Commission. They are the experts in specific policy areas and experts who frequently believe firmly in the need for certain EC policies. They provide the expertise but, perhaps more importantly, the continuity and the tenacity necessary for the development of EC policy. The Commissioner responsible for a specific DG is dependent on the civil servants in it for advice. In the case of social policy, the Commissioner responsible is also, as noted above, generally a person sympathetic to EC action in this sector.

The study of social policy shows the civil servants in the DG for Social Policy acting as an internal interest group to keep alive the possibility of an EC policy on worker participation and programs for women when such policies were out of favor politically, demonstrating an autonomy from political currents. They rewrote and restructured proposals numerous times in a search for a form that would gain acceptance in the Council. They organized conferences to arouse public awareness. In a limited way, they prepared the way for the Social Dimension.

The effectiveness of the bureaucracy since the acceptance of the Social Dimension is demonstrated by the speed with which civil servants have prepared drafts for laws proposed in the Social Dimension. By 1991, drafts exist for most all the proposals for new EC laws contained in the Social Dimension. Civil servants have drafted rapidly complex laws for social policies ranging from worker participation to health and safety. In addition, the proposals have been drafted in such a way as to best ensure their acceptance. (This point is discussed more fully in the chapters that follow, but it refers primarily to efforts by the bureaucracy to draft laws in such a manner that they fall under provisions of the SEA which provide for majority voting in the Council.) The civil servants have involved many national experts and interest group representatives in the drafting process in order to broaden support and to avoid the inclusion of provisions that are unacceptable to important actors. (Many business people would argue that they are not adequately involved in this process.)

Observations based on numerous interviews conducted over a ten-year period in DG V (social policy) lead to the conclusion that a small number of civil servants are responsible for drafting social policy and these individuals are, by training and by personal value systems, committed to the development of a comprehensive EC social policy. They are autonomous from their national governments. Their motivation arises from within the Commission and they constitute an institutional interest group as that concept is used by functionalists.

## DOES EFFECTIVE COMMUNICATION EXIST BETWEEN THE EC AND CITIZENS IN THE MEMBER STATES?

The fourth question concerns whether the EC communicates effectively with the people. Is it mobilizing support and awareness? The Commission, led by Jacques Delors, has made a strong effort to inform citizens about the Social Dimension. Much of the effort has been directed at labor unions. Commissioners regularly appear at large union conferences. The DG for Information (DG X) has a special section for labor unions which maintains a variety of links with labor unions. It publishes a bulletin for them. It invites delegations of trade unionists to Brussels and its civil servants cultivate ties with labor leaders. The Commission also funds projects such as conferences and the research arm of the ETUC, the European Trade Union Institute.

It is difficult to ascertain how effective the Commission is in communicating to citizens and mobilizing support. Poll results offer one possible indicator. *Eurobarometer* carries on polls to measure popular support for integration. The findings indicate that Europeans support both integration and 1992. However, support for 1992 has declined from a high of 57 percent in 1987 to 45 percent in 1990 (CEC 1990i: 1). Support is highest among professional and business people and lowest among the working class. Significantly, support is higher among Europeans for the social dimension than it is for 1992. The Commission, no doubt, is aware of this fact and recognizes the importance of success in the social area to success in the economic area. Sixty-four percent of the people polled in spring 1990 were favorable toward the controversial charter for social rights (CEC 1990i: 22).

Support in the United Kingdom was above the EC average, despite the fact that the British government opposed the charter. (It was the only government to do so.) However, further examination of polls indicates that caution should be exercised before drawing conclusions regarding the Commission's success in mobilizing popular support for social policy. A majority of respondents in another poll believed that the national level is the appropriate level to make policies on health and safety and on worker participation. These same respondents believed that the EC is the appropriate level to make such important policies as foreign policy and environmental policy (CEC 1990i: 27). It would seem that people who generally support integration still want to preserve social policy—which is so personally important to them—at the level more familiar to them.

It appears that a lag exists between the orientation of interest groups and some elites and the citizens in the member countries. European employees have had decades of experience with national policies that protect them. These national policies have not yet been replaced by EC policies. Neither is it obvious to employees, at this time, that the creation of the internal market is undercutting the effectiveness of national policies. Interest groups and elites may perceive that it will, but they are not being activated by employee demands. Europeans like the ideal of integration but they want the security of known national programs. As in the case of interest groups and elites, the study of popular response to EC social policy indicates that the crucial transfer of loyalty may be linked to both the perception of the inadequacy of nation action and the reality of EC action. At the present time, neither of these factors exists for the people in the EC. Citizens still depend on national policies, and relevant EC policies are not yet functioning. In the terminology of functionalism, evidence does not exist to demonstrate that the Social Dimension has resulted in advances in political socialization among the people in the member states.

## DOES THE EC HAVE POLITICAL STRUCTURES TO PERFORM POLITICAL FUNCTIONS?

The fifth question is concerned with the extent to which the EC has structures to perform political functions. Since this study focuses primarily on current and proposed policies, insights can be provided only for policy making. Comments regarding policy implementation and adjudication are not possible at this early stage. Certainly researchers in the years ahead will be interested in studying how the Commission will function to ensure the implementation of social policies—especially those that require significant modifications in customary practices. Researchers should also find the role of the Court in adjudicating the many legal questions raised by the passage of social policies a fertile field of study. As discussed in following chapters, the Commission is stretching the interpretation of some articles in the SEA in order to place proposed social policies under provisions of the Treaty which require only a qualified majority vote in the Council. The British government has already promised to challenge this practice.

The politics of the social dimension reveal some interesting developments in the EC policy-making process. The bargaining process is being revised significantly as a result of changes put in place by the SEA, as well as by the greater political salience of social issues in contrast to the technical matters which are typically the subject of EC policies. The institutions of the EC are adjusting their roles in response to the challenge of the Social Dimension and also in response to the opportunities offered by the SEA. However, the institutions are not exercising distinct political functions to indicate increasing integration as defined by functionalism.

The Commission is the premier player in the social dimension. It is both initiator and lobbyist. It serves to aggregate the interest of business and labor into proposals that will satisfy diverse demands and also to increase the legitimacy of the EC with Europeans. There is no doubt that one of the main purposes of the Social Dimension is to increase popular support for the EC, European integration, and 1992. The Commission has been cautious to draft proposals so that they are not subject to vehement opposition by important groups, especially business groups. No definitive confrontation has yet taken place to test the commitment of the Commission to the Social Dimension versus its commitment to 1992. Evidence indicates, however, that the Commission casts the Social Dimension in the supporting role.

The study of the politics of the social dimension does not reveal many significant developments regarding the evolution of the Parliament. Parliament supports the Social Dimension as it has supported most social policies in the past. Political parties in the Parliament show some independence from their national political party counterparts. They are more "European" and more supportive of social policies. Members of Parliament (MEPs), seeking a meaningful role for Parliament in the formation of EC social policies, have joined with other MEPs on positions that are at variance with their national political party and even with their own government. For example, MEPs from the British Conservative party were instrumental in revising the Vredeling proposal and gaining its acceptance in Parliament at a time when the Thatcher government was vehemently opposed to it (Springer 1987).

The Parliament had three small victories regarding social policy in recent years: 1) requesting the right to cooperation with the Council on social matters which it was granted; 2) blocking a proposed directive on health and safety when the Council failed to obtain unanimity to override the Parliament; and 3) passing a resolution which encouraged the Commission to draft a framework directive on health and safety at work. Optimists may see in the victories seeds that promise further developments that will make the Parliament a locus for interest aggregation by European political parties and for a meaningful role as a convertor of European demands into EC policies. Realists should, perhaps, await the outcome of the intergovernmental conference which is writing a treaty that may give the Parliament a broader legal base for the expansion of its role.

The politics of the social dimension in the Council is characterized by a steady division between the British and all the rest. (Now that Margaret Thatcher can no longer be relied on for a veto on social policies, other divisions may appear.) Because the British position was one of almost complete opposition to the development of EC social policies, advocates of such policies found means to bypass the British and the British lost bargaining power as a result. As mentioned previously, the Commission drafted measures under provisions of the SEA that permit the use of a qualified majority vote in the Council. Members of the Council, with the exception of the British, have not protested this practice, with important consequences for the future. They also accept the use of forms such as resolutions in place of directives for the same reason. The Social Dimension was passed as a resolution with the support of eleven members.

The enlargement of the EC and the passage of the SEA combined make the Council a more cooperative partner for the Commission regarding social issues. The enlargement of the EC brings together the Council leaders, such as Filipe Gonzalez, who share the interest of the Commission regarding the Social Dimension. The Council now can be depended upon to provide the necessary qualified majority for many social proposals. Recent European Council meetings, such as the ones held during both the French and the Spanish presidencies, have been used by sympathetic leaders in order to highlight social policy. The extent to which the partnership may go has not been tested, however. Most Council members accept that extension of the EC competency to include social policy, but they have not yet been called upon to accept a policy that would entail a significant and public loss of national sovereignty over a program. The Commission has avoided politics of confrontation. Its style continues to be the politics of incrementalism characteristic of function-alism. The power of the Council remains preeminent, but the power of individual members of the Council has been lessened. The restraint on individual members, coupled with the acceptance of the Council of a social dimension to 1992, may be seen as a small step toward European integration.

## CONCLUSION

The politics of the social dimension offer an interesting case study of the process of European integration. The concepts of functionalist theory are useful to analyze the process. The study shows that the 1992 initiative led to a spillover effect for the enlargement of EC competency in the social sphere. The acceptance of the Social Dimension, in turn, has led to increased European politics. Elites, interest groups, and governments now regard the EC as a legitimate level for policies that go well beyond the original economic objectives. The inability of member states to respond to the demands of both business and labor leaders was an important factor in compelling the shift.

The study shows that the major institutions of the EC have made small changes in their traditional roles. They have not achieved the distinct separation of functions foreseen by functionalists that would indicate a high level of integration. The Commission functions as both an initiator of policy and an interest group promoting integration measures. It has gained stature and become the focus for European politics largely through the strength of its present leadership. The Parliament has gained a modicum of authority but continues to lack the power that would make it an arena for true interest aggregation by unified European political parties. The study of the Council reveals the importance of the SEA in lessening the power of any one member state to follow a politics of obstruction. The SEA makes alliance building among its members more essential and it also opens up a greater potential for coalition building among members of the Council and the Commission.

The findings in the case study support the conclusion of Juliet Lodge in a recent book. She concluded that a significant shift has occurred among Europeans who now regard the EC as the legitimate arena for many types of policies. She calls this the quiet revolution of the 1980s and predicts that it will continue into the 1990s (Lodge 1989: 328).

*Chapter 6*

# What 1992 Means for European Women

The European Community (EC) has placed working women into a special category in employment policies since its first social action program in 1974. Although women's issues have never occupied a prominent place in its work, the EC has been instrumental in advancing the interests of working women.

Women comprise one-third of the work force in the EC. They are a permanent and growing part of that work force, so the effect of 1992 on women in the work force needs separate consideration. Preliminary evidence indicates that women may be more at risk by the formation of the single market than are male employees. The single market may pose a threat both to the jobs which women have and to the laws which protect them.

This chapter will be divided into five parts. The first three will provide the necessary background, including a profile of women in the work force in the EC, information on relevant national policies, and a summary of previous EC policies. The remaining parts contain an explanation of the problems posed by the 1992 initiative for working women and an examination of the response of the EC to those problems.

## PROFILE OF WOMEN IN THE WORK FORCE IN THE EC

Women entered the work force in Western Europe in increasing numbers throughout the postwar era, even in the 1970s when the participation rate for men began to fall. Women between the ages of fifteen and fifty-nine now normally have a job or are looking for one. In Denmark, 75.9 percent of adult women were employed in 1987. Spain had the lowest participation rate in the EC with 37.5 percent of adult women at work (Jackson 1990: 5). Women most commonly work in the service sector. Indeed, 76.4 percent of them find their jobs in that sector (CEC 1989p: 124). Women are also most likely to work in feminized work places. They are bank tellers, nurses, teachers, and cleaners in hotels. They are unlikely to be bank managers, executives in private business, well-paid technicians, or hotel managers. Women who work in industry tend to be concentrated in a few sectors which are less well paid and more labor intensive, such as the clothing and textile industry. The situation in Germany illustrates the fact of segregation. Ninety percent of working women find their jobs in only twelve occupational categories (CEC 1989k: 87). Women also fill a disproportionate number of part-time jobs; for example, they provide 90 percent of the part-time work force in Germany (CEC 1989v: 72). According to the latest report, 28.6 percent of women's employment is part-time (CEC 1989p: 140). Working women in the EC still have not achieved equality in pay or opportunity despite laws requiring equality. Women's pay is probably 31 percent less than men's (Jackson 1990: 50). However, pay scales differ greatly among the member states. What women want and what society expects for women also varies among the member states. For example, a French woman employed in a bank has a much greater chance of reaching a managerial position than does her British counterpart. Also the French woman is much more likely to find a place in a good public nursery for her child than her British counterpart, and both the British and the French woman would expect more social acceptance for their careers than would a female bank employee in Portugal.

## NATIONAL POLICIES FOR WOMEN IN THE WORK FORCE

The governments of all of the member states of the EC have laws to protect and assist working women. In addition, the governments have created high-level agencies or even ministries for women's issues. The old paternalistic laws, such as those banning women from night work, have gradually given way to more modern laws on equal treatment. Discrimination is illegal in all countries, but the definition of discrimination varies considerably, as does the quality of enforcement (Landau 1985). A 1983 French law requires employers to make an annual report about their personnel policies for women. The law provides sanctions for transgressions as well as protections for an employee making charges against an employer (France 1984: 487). In general, most governments have been more effective in banning overt discrimination than in devising policies for affirmative action.

Working mothers have more assistance from the law in EC countries than they have in the United States. Every country has a law which provides for maternity leave. Italian women are entitled to twenty weeks of paid leave but British women to only six. In all countries, employers may not fire a regular employee because of pregnancy or refuse to allow a woman to return to work following maternity leave. Parental leave is also beginning to appear in some countries. Most countries have inadequate public provisions for child care, but the French government provides a good system of public child care centers. That system may be a factor in explaining why French women are more likely to remain in the work force during childbearing years than are women in most other EC countries (OECD 1985: 34).

New public policies for women are being devised in response to unemployment and to changes in the work place. Schools are encouraging girls to consider a variety of careers. Training programs are being reformed so that women may participate more easily. A great deal of research is being conducted in order to ascertain what is needed in order to better use women in the work force. The efforts are scattered and sporadic, but governments are increasingly accepting responsibility to assure that women have the preparation needed for modern job opportunities.

## THE DEVELOPMENT OF EC POLICIES FOR WOMEN

The right of the EC to formulate a policy for working women derives from the Treaty of Rome. Article 119 establishes the principle of equal pay for men and women. The preamble to the treaty as well as Articles 117 to 122 give the EC a general grant of power for social policy.

The 1970s was the decade when the EC began to address women's issues. It was a period when both the Council of Ministers and the Commission had leaders who were sympathetic to the social concerns of the day. Equality, workers' rights, and social justice were values which found their way onto the political agendas of the countries of Western Europe and onto the agenda of the EC. The Social Action Program of 1974 was the result. The program promised action "to achieve equality between men and women as regards access to employment and vocational training and advancement and as regards working conditions including pay" (CEC 1974b). The statement constituted the first elaboration of the meaning of Article 119 and laid the foundation for the EC to act over a broad range of job rights for women.

The EC quickly started to fulfill its commitment by enacting three directives on equal rights at work. They were the Equal Pay Directive of 1975, the Equal Treatment Directive of 1976, and the Social Security Directive of 1978. The meaning of each directive has been broadened by subsequent rulings of the European Court, but most member states have been remiss in enforcing them. Today the definition of equal pay in the EC means equal pay for work of equal value. Equal treatment now makes illegal all forms of sex discrimination at work including hiring, training, and promotion. Most importantly, it protects women against both direct and indirect discrimination. The directive on social security applies to both national social security systems and special occupational and supplementary schemes. It does not require uniformity among the national programs, and it allows those programs to contain special benefits for women. It protects women against provisions which are discriminatory even when the discrimination is indirect (CEC 1983).

The organization of the Commission was changed in the 1970s in response to the new interest in women's issues. The units added continue to be responsible for EC policies for women. The equal opportunities unit in the Directorate General for Employment, Social Affairs, and Education (DG V) carries on the bulk of the work. A handful of civil servants are responsible for the information gathering, analysis, and consulting necessary for preparing and overseeing policies for working women. DG V is under the direction of the commissioner who holds the portfolio for social affairs. (In 1991, the commissioner responsible for social affairs was Vasso Papandreou. She was the first woman in that position and one of the only two women ever to be a commissioner.) A women's information service operates in the Directorate General for Information, Communication and Culture (DG X). It is responsible for disseminating information about women and publishes a series called *Women of Europe*. The European Parliament and the Economic and Social Committee have special committees to deal with women's issues. Both institutions have advocated a strong EC policy for women. The Court of Justice has also played a role in developing the EC policy for women through a liberal interpretation of EC law.

The scope and ambition of the EC policy for working women developed in the 1970s is quite remarkable. The policy contains both legal measures to ban discrimination and nonlegal measures to facilitate the social and psychological changes necessary for true equality. Traditional family values intermingle with newer feminist concerns in a broad range of initiatives. For example, the Commission sponsored seminars to encourage bankers to be less sexist in their personnel policies. The Commission studied vocational education in order to ascertain why women remain in feminized work places. The Commission delved into the question of the relationship between family responsibilities and success in the work place. The EC used the Social Fund to provide training for women to enter jobs formerly inaccessible to them. During the formative period of the 1970s, the EC chose an activist approach which surpassed merely formulating measures essential to harmonize national policies which might have inhibited competition in the internal market.

In 1981, the disparate EC activities for women were brought together in the first action program to promote equal opportunities for women. The opening sentence of the document states, "The Community's longstanding commitment to the improvement of the situation of women has established it as a pioneer and innovator in this field" (CEC 1981). The rest of the document does not match the bold opening sentence. Discussion in the document is brief and focuses primarily on the problems working women were facing because of the recession. Member governments were given the primary responsibility of alleviating the problems.

The annex of the document contains sixteen proposals for legal and nonlegal measures to promote equality. In almost every case, the responsibility for action is divided between the EC and the member state. Frequently, the role of the EC is only to study the situation and then consider action; however, six of the proposals fit into the activist mold of the 1970s. They are:

1. An EC law on equal treatment for women in occupational, social security schemes.
2. An EC law on equal treatment for self-employed women and women in agriculture.
3. An EC law on parental leave and leave for family reasons, and on the building of public services and facilities to assist working parents.
4. Possible legislation on pregnancy and motherhood if the Commission considers it necessary.
5. Future legislation on steps needed for action to assist women in achieving equal opportunity.

6. Extension of EC action on vocational education so women can participate in new technological sectors through the Social Fund and the center for vocational training in Berlin.

The dates for the action program, 1982-1985, coincided with the period when the integration appeared stalled and economic problems took precedence. Only the first two proposals listed above became law according to the schedule given in the program (CEC 1984b); however, the other proposals remained on the agenda of the Commission.

A second action program appeared in 1985, when Europessimism was strongest. It was also the year when the EC was deeply involved with two historic documents: the White Paper on Completing the Internal Market and the Single European Act. Seen against that time, the second action program is quite remarkable. Although it contains no major new programs, it is a thoughtful and interesting document. It shows the influence of research conducted in the Commission over the past decade. Emphasis is given to the psychological dimension of discrimination. The writers of the document doubted the efficacy of laws to end discrimination. Ways to change attitudes, and not just attitudes in the work place, were needed. The basis of discrimination is in society and in the family. The sharing of family responsibility is listed as the sine qua non for true equality (CEC 1986b: 5). Many of the proposals in the document reflect this orientation, such as the proposal for a campaign to increase public awareness. Other proposals were a reiteration of some in the first action program, which still await acceptance. Four proposals were to become focal points of controversy. They are:

1. A legal instrument to facilitate action by women against employers who discriminate. The instrument was to be based on the principle of the reversal of the burden of proof.
2. A code of practice on positive actions which should guide employers and member states in order to facilitate providing equal opportunity.
3. A measure to protect working women during pregnancy and motherhood.
4. A directive on parental leave and leave for family reasons.

Although the overall document is positive, the difficulties of the 1980s color it in several ways. The fact that many of the proposals were in the first program shows that the EC failed to gain acceptance for them as scheduled. The emphasis on cheap psychological campaigns rather than on programs which would require large budgets probably resulted from the EC being on the verge of bankruptcy at the time. Finally, the document contains a passage which was to be reproduced in many proposals over the next few years. It states, "The Commission firmly believes that this objective [equal opportunity] may be achieved without imposing any unreasonable burden on industry or on small- and medium-size enterprises in particular" (p. 3).

## THE EFFECT OF 1992 ON WORKING WOMEN

As has been seen in previous chapters, the goal of the single market is to create a large economy with sophisticated, competitive enterprises. Such a goal assumes the restructuring and rationalization of industries. It also assumes the availability of a flexible, skilled work force. No one can know all the ramifications of the changes. The troublesome fact, however, is that little was done in the early stages of planning to anticipate how those changes would affect women. Women have special problems under current employment conditions and may be more vulnerable to modernization in the work place. Will the consolidation of the single market worsen the situation for working women, and what concerns may the EC have about the employment of women? One needs to analyze the relevant documents to answer those questions. Finally, one should also look at proposals which the EC is considering and will probably issue in the next few years.

The examination of the basic documents of the 1992 initiative in earlier chapters showed that social issues are only dealt with tangentially as they relate to needs of the single market, so women's issues were not mentioned in those documents although they have a relevance for women. The Single European Act is important for women primarily because it reforms the decision-making process to give more importance to the European Parliament. Parliament not only has more power, it also is more visible. The Council can only disregard the opinion of Parliament on most matters through a unanimous vote. The Commission generally works closely with relevant members of Parliament when drafting new proposals. Even the media no longer ignore the Parliament. The Parliament which was elected in 1989 is sympathetic to the concerns of working women. A parliamentary committee on women's rights pressures the Commission and Council to expedite proposals of interest to women and to consider new areas of action. In the spring of 1990, for example, the Council passed a Communication to the Commission urging it to draft a directive on child care.

The Single European Act does not mention women. It is primarily a document for reforming the institutions and their powers and not a document for human rights. It does however include a reference to the fundamental rights of freedom, equality, and social justice in its preamble. The only mention of rights in the body of the document is the requirement that proposals dealing with the rights of employed persons shall be excluded from majority voting in the Council (Article 100 A). The amendment of Article 118, allowing a qualified majority vote in the Council on directives dealing with health and safety in the work place, is also important for women. Many jobs which women perform involve health risks, especially if they are pregnant. The only other part of the Single European Act that directly concerns women is Article 130 A-E which reforms the Social Fund. The Social Fund, which had assisted a number of programs important to women, is now incorporated into a Structural Fund in order to strengthen economic and social cohesion.

The White Paper on Completing the Internal Market deals with social issues only as they relate to the needs of a free labor market and does not mention women. It does, however, state that the Commission will consult with governments and the social partners about appropriate measures to fulfill "the Community's employment and social security objectives" (CEC 1985b: 8). It also contains an admission that social risks may be associated with the completion of the internal market, so funds to alleviate negative consequences will be enhanced. Such an admission is minor in a document which is primarily economic and which conveys an optimistic impression of the vast benefits to be gained from the completion of the internal market.

Three years after the White Paper, the Commission published the document known as the Social Dimension (CEC 1988k), which contains a discussion of the social problems which may emerge from the formation of the internal market. It also contains a list of proposed solutions. The document echoes the optimism about the benefits of the market found in the White Paper, as shown in the following quote from the foreword: "Through greater efficiency of the machinery of production . . . the internal market will make it possible to develop growth potential and thus to improve working conditions, employment prospects and, in short, the standard of living of Europeans in general" (p. vi). The document goes on to assure employees that the social protection which they currently enjoy will not be called into question. However, the primary message is that the Social Dimension "is not in opposition to nor must it slow down the completion of the internal market" (p. vii).

Women are dealt with in the document in one short section which makes reference to the second action program for women. It states that the action program will be assessed in 1989 and proposals will be made on the basis of the assessment (p. 56). The list of proposals found in the annex of the paper contains a number of proposals of special interest to women. The most directly relevant are:

1. The creation of the IRIS program for the vocational training of women.
2. A health and safety directive to protect persons who work with video display units.
3. A program to help women set up businesses.
4. A directive to assure equal treatment for women in social security programs.
5. A recommendation on sharing family and work responsibilities.
6. A directive on establishing the burden of proof in sex discrimination cases.
7. A directive on parental leave.
8. A code of practice on maternity protection.
9. A program to monitor family policies.
10. A program on positive action to increase occupational mobility for women.

If all those proposals were implemented, they would protect and a..ist women in dealing with the changes arising from the formation of the internal market, but two factors mitigate the possibility that the proposals will be implemented. Compliance with some of the proposals would be voluntary because they do not have the force of law as directives and regulations do. Other proposals, such as the recommendation on sharing family and work responsibilities, only establish a moral standard or a vague principle. Recently, the EC has resorted to the use of recommendations and resolutions for proposals for social policy in an effort to find a middle ground between the demands from labor unions and the opposition from employers and the British government. The second obstacle to the implementation of the proposals arises from most social policies requiring the unanimous approval of the Council, and the British government opposes social action by the EC. Only measures which are necessary to the internal market may be enacted by a qualified majority vote in the Council. The only social proposals which unquestionably fall under the internal market are those affecting health and safety. The EC is thus making great progress in establishing an ambitious health and safety policy, but the innocent-appearing recommendation on sharing family and work responsibilities failed in the Council solely because of a British veto.

A common thread links the proposals for a social dimension and the two action programs for women. Indeed, all of the main proposals for women contained in the former trace directly to discussions in the first action program. The EC has reiterated a commitment to working women through three major policy documents in the 1980s. However, the fact that proposals made in a document written in 1981 were still being proposed in a document issued seven years later show that the Commission has not succeeded in overcoming opposition in the EC. The only exceptions to this generalization are the two directives proposed in the first action program and accepted in 1986. One is on equal treatment for women and women in occupational, social security schemes. The other is on equal treatment for men and women employed in an activity, including agriculture, in a self-employed capacity, and on the protection of self-employed women during pregnancy and motherhood (CEC 1986a).

The proposals in the first action program were designed to achieve equality for working women when: " . . . the majority of working women are in precarious forms of employment, notably the unskilled sector and part-time and temporary work. . . . The situation for women is exacerbated by the effects of public expenditure cuts on social infrastructure . . . and by the introduction of manpower-saving technologies in areas . . . where female labor is preponderant" (CEC 1981: 3).

The situation for working women today is much the same as it was when the first action program was written. The internal market may make more vulnerable those women who are still in "precarious forms of employment" and accelerate the introduction of manpower-saving technologies, so policies proposed for the conditions of the early 1980s are still relevant. The crucial need is not the elaboration of new policies but the implementation of ones proposed almost a decade ago.

In 1989 the major controversy over social policy centered on the proposed Social Charter (CEC 1989c). It is the most important document on social policy since the Social Dimension. The document is important because it establishes the principle that the employee rights listed in the document are norms which all member states should respect. The Charter contains only a simple provision for women stating that equal treatment for women and men shall be guaranteed and equal opportunities shall be developed. The Germans tried to add a right to maternity leave but were not successful. The Charter invokes the principle of subsidiarity. Primary responsibility for social measures remains with the member governments and the social partners. The EC will act only when a need exists for a common policy, raising questions about the future of the EC policy for working women.

The Charter was followed by an action program which contains proposals to implement the rights established by the Charter (CEC 1989b). The action program also includes a comprehensive survey of the status of previous proposals. According to the survey, no policy about women, except the two previously mentioned, had been accepted by November 1989. Only the proposal on video display units appeared ripe for acceptance. The program also contains four "new initiatives" for women, but none is truly new (p. 38). They are: A third action program for women, a directive on the protection of pregnant women at work, a recommendation about child care, and a recommendation for a code of conduct for the protection of pregnancy and maternity leave for working women.

The document also provides the information that two other proposed directives important to women are due for change. Both the proposed directives on part-time work and on temporary work have been withdrawn. (They were blocked by the British in the Council.) According to the document, the two proposals would be replaced by a single one for atypical forms of work. In June 1990, a new version appeared with three parts, each falling under a different treaty provision (CEC 1990k). (The new proposals are discussed more fully in Chapter 8.)

The only new aspect in the EC policy for women to be added in the 1980s is not included in the action program which accompanies the Charter. Sexual harassment is a problem which the Commission is just starting to consider. The Commission had a study made on the topic in 1988 (CEC 1988l). The study shows that member governments have not dealt adequately with the problem. The Commission is expected to issue early in the 1990s a directive on sexual harassment.

Late in 1990, the Commission adopted a third action program for women. It is for 1991 to 1995. According to the initial CREW assessment, the program, as accepted, is much weaker than was the original draft made in DG V (CREW 1990b). The program contains a few areas of emphasis that could be important. The Commission promises to work to ensure that member states enforce existing laws. It also promises to produce a code of conduct on sexual harassment and guidelines on the principle of equal pay for work of equal value. These are incremental developments that continue the pattern of recent Commission policy for women.

The review of the EC policy for women leads to three conclusions:

1. The EC has an ambitious agenda of proposals for women.
2. The EC has not made any major new proposals for women as a result of the 1992 initiative.
3. Progress in implementing the proposals for women continues to be slow in contrast to the speed with which progress is being made on the 1992 initiative.

In order to determine if the existing policy for women will be adequate in the face of changes associated with the internal market, one needs to try to foresee those changes and relate them to the special characteristics of women's work.

## WOMEN'S WORK AND 1992

Although no definitive study exists on how the job market will change as a result of 1992, certain types of changes can be anticipated. With open borders and increased competition, weak firms will either go bankrupt or be taken over. All firms will face strong pressure to cut costs, meaning that they will seek means to use their work force more productively. Large firms will restructure. They may locate operations where the work force is most suitable for their needs, either in terms of training or costs. The entire EC economy will become more service and high technology dependent. Agriculture and traditional industries will be under heavy pressure to modernize. The entire economy will grow faster.

The growth will destabilize the labor market. Job creation and job destruction will occur but not necessarily in tandem or in the same regions of the EC. Job skills will be outmoded and new ones will be needed. The changes will require a work force which is flexible, willing to move to where jobs are being created and willing to learn new skills. Such demands for flexibility will be serious for working people. At least for the immediate future, the scenario promises insecurity and disruption, even though a skilled and mobile person will probably find increased opportunities.

The question is where do women fit into the scenario? The tentative answer must be sought by comparing the current profile of women in the work force with the expected changes. The comparison must also take into consideration the special features of work life for women. Women's work in the EC today has the following characteristics:

1. Primarily in the service sector.
2. Concentrated in jobs with low skill requirements.
3. A large proportion of the underground or black economy.
4. More often in small- or medium-sized firms than men's work.
5. More often in atypical work (part-time, short-term contract, or seasonal) than men's work.

In addition to the above characteristics of women's work, certain sociological features of working women are also relevant in considering their vulnerability to changes associated with the 1992 initiative. They are:

1. A significant proportion of the female work force is composed of women with dependent children.
2. Family responsibilities may make women less mobile.
3. Women spend more time on housework than do men.
4. Women tend to limit their job search to a narrow range of jobs commonly regarded as "women's work," such as the textile industry or health care.
5. Women generally have lower education and skill levels than men and less often benefit from training programs.
6. In 1989, the unemployment rate for women in the EC was 13 percent compared to 8 percent for men.

On the basis of the information above, certain tentative conclusions are possible. Women who work in many of the feminized work places in the EC face a high probability of unemployment. Research carried out for the EC indicates that about forty industries will be highly sensitive to competitive pressures associated with 1992. Women are a significant proportion of the employees in half of those industries. Indeed, 1.6 million women work in just six of them (Jackson 1990: 26). Women who hold vulnerable jobs generally lack the skills and possibly the mobility for other jobs. They are frequently constrained by tradition and family responsibilities from taking advantage of the opportunities offered in the new market. The implementation of the EC proposals on training and on child care would help to alleviate the vulnerability (The Department of Labour 1990).

Despite recent job creation, unemployment among women appears to be increasing although the participation rate continues to climb. A report by the Commission concludes that the rise in female unemployment is a sign of structural problems arising from job segregation. The trend can only be reversed by specific measures to assist women (CEC 1988m). As industries such as textiles and electronics modernize, women lose the jobs which are outmoded and men obtain the new, highly skilled jobs (EP 1988b). If women are to break out of this unemployment problem, they must have training for the new jobs.

The Commission made training the priority in the Social Dimension. The amount of money for training in the Social Fund increased, but programs for training women were no longer a priority in the Social Fund as they had been in the 1970s. Women's advocates protested those changes (CREW 1989). The only new training program for women in the action program which accompanies the Social Charter is the IRIS program, which has the smallest budget of any current training programs (CEC 1989q: Annex A).

In 1989 the Commission appeared ready to respond to demands regarding training for women, but the Council was less responsive. The Commission requested that the EC center for vocational education study equal opportunity in training. The report from the center states, "During the 1980s training for women inside and outside the companies was too inadequate in quantity and quality to respond to demand in an even remotely coherent manner" (CEDEFOP 1989: 8). The same month the report was issued, the Council passed a resolution on vocational education which did not mention women. In 1990, the EC gave provisional approval to an important training program for women which promises to make training for women once again a priority in the Social Fund. The program is called New Opportunities for Women and is known by its initials NOW. The program is to have a budget of 120 million ECU (1 ECU = US $1.15 in 1990) (CREW 1990a).

Firms are expected to face increased pressure to contain costs in the new, more competitive market. Marginal firms and those producing labor-intensive products may seek to contain labor costs by moving to the south of Europe where labor costs are less. Labor laws are the weakest, and the black economy is also the strongest in Southern Europe. Governments there need foreign investment, so they may hesitate to upgrade their laws or take steps to eradicate the black economy. If "social dumping" takes place and firms move in search of weak labor laws, then women, who are already in the underground economy, could be trapped in jobs which compete with those in third world countries. Commissioner

Vasso Papandreou said in a speech to a British labor union conference, "There is a real danger of reinforcing the segregation of the labor market. We must take care that women do not disappear from the regular labor market into concealed or marginal jobs in the black economy" (CEC 1989t). Two proposals in the action program which accompanies the Social Charter are directly applicable to the problems. One is the proposed directive on atypical work. The other is a directive now being drafted for a document on proof of employment. The latter is being designed to assure legal status for employees in the black economy as a step toward ending it.

The competitive pressures of 1992 seem to be intensifying trends toward using part-time or temporary labor. About 14 percent of total employment in the EC is part-time and 40 percent of the jobs created in the EC since 1985 are part-time. Women comprise the vast majority of part-time employees as well as a significant proportion of the total in atypical work. According to the 1989 Employment in Europe, the increase in atypical work negatively affects women's employment (CEC 1989l: 87). In many cases, women are caught in these jobs, not by choice but by necessity. The proposed policy on atypical work may slow the growth of part-time employment by equalizing the costs for employers between part-time and full-time employment. It will also assure that the women holding atypical jobs will enjoy basic protections.

The service sector is where jobs are increasing, and women are benefitting more than men from the increase. Of the 5 million jobs created between 1985 and 1988, women filled 3 million of them (CEC 1990c); however, the quality of some of those jobs is questionable. The growth of the service sector results in part from the externalization of services which were formerly performed by employees of manufacturing firms, such as cleaning services. Jobs which are "externalized" frequently are lower paying and offer fewer promotions than when they were performed by employees in a manufacturing firm. As for the higher level jobs being created in the service additions, women may not benefit equally from them. The example of banks is not encouraging. Women have made few inroads into management despite the large number of women employed by banks. The EC has targeted banks for intensive study of employment patterns for women. The findings of reports made for the EC indicate that traditional attitudes form a barrier to the advancement of women and lead to the conclusion that laws alone will not be adequate to bring change. Positive actions will be necessary (Laufer 1982: 12; Chalude 1982: 98). In 1984 the Council passed a weak recommendation on positive action (CEC 1984a) stating that member states should take steps to eliminate the effects of attitudes and behavior which impede equal opportunity for women and to encourage women to revise their own thinking about employment. The action program which accompanies the Social Charter lists a proposal for an EC program on positive action, but the details of that program have not yet appeared.

## CONCLUSION

EC policy for women followed a pattern of incremental growth after the initial burst of activity in the 1970s. The pattern was not disrupted by the 1992 initiative or by the social dimension. EC policy for women is broadly based and comprised of both laws and efforts to improve the sociological framework in which women work. It encompasses customary laws against discrimination and it also includes measures to assist working women to meet the dual demands of family and work.

The recent initiatives of the Commission for maternity leave and child care are examples of the efforts to provide conditions in which women can satisfy the dual demands of family and work (CEC 1990l).

The proposals currently under consideration in the EC are not new. All have evolved from earlier proposals. All are related to policies and values long familiar in the member states. The policy, considered as a whole, appears broad and ambitious but analysis reveals that it is a cautious mixture of law and sociology marked by a recognition of the limits where EC can have an impact. The findings accord with the conclusion of Sonia Mazey that EC policy for women is a clear example of incremental policy making (Mazey 1988: 63).

The politics of EC policy making for women show the important role of interest groups in keeping alive an issue when political concerns of greater salience threaten to obscure the issue. The most important interest group is a small group of civil servants in the Commission who persisted in efforts to gather information and to build support for an EC policy for women. The group provided a center for contacts among interested national groups as well as with CREW. The strategy was not confrontational. It was, perhaps, not even overt, but the cumulative impact of the work of the institutional interest group, of CREW, and of the national interest groups was to make consideration of 1992 for working women a legitimate part of current EC policy making.

The Parliament played a role as an articulator of the interests of women as well. The Parliament has a number of persons who are highly visible in promoting women's issues. It has a committee that provides a forum for discussions of proposals for women. The work of Parliament in regard to the proposals was frequently covered in the press. The effect of all of the preceding was probably to increase the legitimacy of the EC as a policy maker in the social sector. It probably also increased the pressure on the Council to treat proposals for women with care.

The Commission was the preeminent actor in the making of policy for women. A distinction needs to be made between the roles of the civil servant in the Commission and the commissioners as a group. The civil servants acted as an interest group as well as the initiators of policy. They demonstrated persistence and originality in drafting proposals in order to ensure their acceptance. The commissioners apparently were more cautious and regarded the proposals as instruments to build support in a carefully orchestrated campaign to achieve the objectives of 1992. In this sense, the commissioners served to aggregate the interests expressed by the civil servants with those arising from other actors. The commissioners placed the concerns of women in the agenda of 1992 but they moderated proposals from the civil servants and never made them a priority to impede the acceptance of other objectives.

The EC policy for women continues to evolve with its unique blend of law and sociology. Despite the potential salience of such policy, the topic has been handled in the EC in the nonconfrontational style that characterizes EC policy making. The policy has not yet reached a point where it makes much difference to the lives of working women. It has, however, reached a point where interest groups and some elites regard the EC as a legitimate arena for such policy. It constitutes a very small factor in the accumulation of forces edging Europe toward integration.

*Chapter 7*

# Industrial Democracy: The Social Charter and the European Company Statute

Industrial democracy is one of the most distinctive features of employee policies in the European Community. It is also one of the most elusive for Americans to understand. Industrial democracy has been discussed in the EC for more than twenty years. It has been practiced in some of the member states at least since World War II. The term is often used interchangeably with the term *worker participation*, which refers to the right of employees to participate in policy making in the work place. Participation may simply be the right to be informed, but it may also be a right to share decision-making authority with management on some matters such as personnel issues. Industrial democracy may be used in a broader sense as well, referring to a bill of rights for employees comparable to a bill of rights for citizens.

Although the EC has dealt with a number of proposals involving industrial democracy, only two will be discussed at length in this chapter. They are the Social Charter and the European Company Statute. The former expresses industrial democracy in the form of basic rights for employees. The latter embodies the worker participation model of industrial democracy. Both have caused political controversies in the EC. Both are perceived by proponents of industrial democracy as representing a test case of the commitment of the leaders of the EC to making the EC a people's Europe rather than a businessman's Europe. Both are feared by opponents who perceive them as building blocks of a socialist or interventionist Europe.

The first part of the chapter contains background information on the philosophy and practice of industrial democracy in Western Europe. The second part traces the development of industrial democracy policies in the EC. The third and most important part of the chapter contains an analysis of the two featured policies and some explanation of the politics involved in their passage.

## INDUSTRIAL DEMOCRACY

The philosophical roots of industrial democracy can be found in both socialist and Catholic thinkers in nineteenth-century Europe. It was associated with a general reaction against problems arising from the industrial revolution and excessive individualism. Various groups of socialists developed ideas about economic democracy and worker control. Marxists, anarchists, syndicalists, and guild socialists all believed that workers had fundamental rights which should be exercised in the work place. Socialism was equated with participatory democracy (it was not associated with centralization and planning until after the Soviet revolution).

Certain nineteenth-century Catholic thinkers rejected the individualistic and profit-oriented values associated with the new industrial economy. They also denied that an adversarial relationship between workers and owners was normal. They accepted private ownership and hierarchy in society but believed such a society should be bound together by mutual responsibility and obligation. They denied that wages formed the only tie between owner and worker. A strong paternalistic element characterized their belief; however, the most clear-sighted among them saw the growing power of workers' organizations and sought ways to channel that power into institutions compatible with the Church's view of the social order. As early as 1835, the Catholic social philosopher, Franz von Baader, proposed the establishment of committees of workers within a firm to curtail the power of the boss. In 1890, Pope Leo XIII expressed the growing Church concern with unbridled capitalism in the encyclical *Rerum Novarum*. The rights and needs of workers were recognized by the Church, but the right of private property was also accepted.

The cooperative model, in which workers and owners share the operation of a firm, found its widest discussion in Germany. It later found expression in the constitution of the Weimar Republic. Article 165 states, "The wage-earning and salaried employees are called upon to co-operate, with equal rights and in community with the entrepreneurs, on the regulation of wage and working conditions and on the total economic development of the productive forces." In 1920, Germany passed a Works Council Act which provided for workers to be represented along with representatives of shareholders on supervisory boards of corporations.

In the reform era following World War II, most countries enacted laws to provide for employee rights. Social rights, such as the right to employment and a living wage, were considered as fundamental as political rights, such as freedom of speech. Basic social rights were incorporated in constitutions written in that period as well as in various international conventions. For example, Article 4 of the Italian constitution reads, "The Republic recognizes the right of all citizens to work, and promotes such conditions as will make this right effective." The Bonn Basic Law states in Article 9, Section 3, "The right to form associations to safeguard and improve working and economic conditions is guaranteed to everyone and to all trades and professions." The Spanish constitution provides for worker participation and consultation in Article 129.

In 1961, the Council of Europe, an international organization to which most Western European countries belong, accepted the European Social Charter (a bill of employee rights). The Charter is in the form of an international convention which members of the Council of Europe may ratify. The Charter has become important in recent years in discussions about an EC social charter.

Most Western European countries provide for worker participation and require one of the following models:

1. Appointment of employee representatives to the supervisory board of companies with the two-tier system (supervisory and management boards), or to the administrative board if the companies operate with a single board. The provision for employee representatives is found in Denmark, France, Germany, and The Netherlands.

2. Selection of employee representatives to a workers' council which has legally defined rights to company information and consultation. Such rights are required in France, Germany, The Netherlands, Belgium, Luxembourg, Spain, and Portugal.

3. Employers and labor unions have the right to negotiate an agreement stipulating employee involvement. That right exists in Ireland, Denmark, Italy, and the United Kingdom.

Today, industrial democracy is a widely accepted norm in Western Europe. It is expressed both in the sense that employees have basic social rights and in the practice of worker participation. National governments and international organizations promote industrial democracy. European employees assume that certain basic rights will be respected by employers.

## INDUSTRIAL DEMOCRACY POLICIES IN THE EC

The 1960s and early 1970s was a period of social ferment when Europeans experimented with many types of democratic reforms. Laws requiring industrial democracy were made more rigorous in many countries. The EC could not stay outside that ferment. Many thought the time had arrived for the EC to strengthen its democratic credentials and become more relevant for ordinary citizens. Others were concerned that different practices of industrial democracy in the member states would interfere with competition in the EC by adding an unequal burden on corporations operating in countries with more costly forms of industrial democracy. The Commission set to work to draft an acceptable EC policy on industrial democracy. Few realized what a long and controversial task it would be.

The first two proposals to include provisions for industrial democracy were the European Company Statute and the Fifth Directive on Company Law. Both proposals had as their primary purpose the reform of company law. Provisions for employee participation were added almost as an afterthought. The European Company Statute, which will be discussed in the following section, was on the agenda of the Council ready for acceptance in early 1973. It quietly disappeared from view when the new British member began to participate.

The Fifth Directive attracted a great deal of attention in the 1970s. The proposal was part of a series of directives designed to harmonize and modernize company laws in the member states. Persons drafting the proposal believed that a requirement for worker participation needed to be included for both philosophical and economic reasons. They called worker participation a democratic imperative, but they could not find a form of worker participation which all parties would accept. They preferred the German codetermination model, but many of the relevant parties did not accept it. The proposal was in the form of a directive, enabling the drafters to include several alternative forms of worker participation so that member governments could select a form most compatible with national norms. Despite numerous revisions and continuing work, the Council has never accepted the Fifth Directive.

The failure of either the European Company Statute or the Fifth Directive to be enacted by the EC primarily resulted from disagreement in the Council; however, the European labor movement was also divided. The European Trade Union Confederation was formed in 1973 to be the voice of labor in the EC. Most of the national labor confederations in Western Europe belong to it. The ETUC established a good working relationship with the Commission and was able to promote social concerns in the EC, but the members of the ETUC were divided on the issue of industrial democracy. The British Trade Union Congress was suspicious of any law which might undermine the traditions of collective bargaining in the United Kingdom. They regarded German codetermination as a device by employers to co-opt workers. Other unions, such as the Belgian, rejected codetermination on ideological grounds: workers should not support a policy which justified capitalism. (The opponents of the EC proposals ironically included trade unionists, who rejected the proposals as a sellout to capitalists, and American capitalists who warned that the proposals threatened the very basis of capitalism.) The search for an acceptable form for industrial democracy in the ETUC succeeded no more than it did in the EC in the 1970s.

While the EC did not succeed in designing a European model of industrial democracy in the 1970s, it did succeed in winning agreement for employee rights using a different approach. That approach side-stepped the issue of a form of participation and assumed that the essence of industrial democracy was not in any form, but rather in giving to employees the legal right to be informed and consulted about corporate decisions which affected them. That right was important to employees in a period when unemployment was growing at rates unknown since the Depression. Support for disclosure rights, which seemed to many to be elementary justice, became so widespread that one authority referred to it as a "disclosure bandwagon" (Peel 1979: 122). The ETUC was united in support of disclosure rights.

In the 1970s, the EC enacted two directives which included disclosure rights. Neither aroused much controversy. A 1975 directive on collective redundancies requires member states to have a law that requires firms considering reductions in the work force to inform employees and consult with them about the reduction (CEC 1975a). It is the first EC legislation to require a "social plan" in which a firm must prepare a study on ways to lessen the harmful effect of a proposed layoff. The provision is modeled on German law. A 1977 directive requires firms to inform and consult employees when a change of ownership takes place. It applies to acquisitions, mergers, and takeovers of businesses or parts of a business.

If the change will affect the work force, the employer must consult the employees "in good time on such measures with a view to seeking agreement" (CEC 1977).

The easy passage of the two directives on disclosure led the Commission to assume that a further directive building on the same base would find similar acceptance. The Commissioner for Employment, Social Affairs, and Education in 1980 was a former Dutch trade union leader named Henk Vredeling. He believed that a directive was needed to ensure that multinational corporations did not escape from the disclosure laws which bound domestic firms. For example, Ford Motor Company had recently closed an operation in The Netherlands without informing employees as early as required by Dutch law. The local managers claimed that they themselves did not know about corporate plans at an earlier date. Only corporate headquarters had known and it was beyond the reach of Dutch law.

The Vredeling proposal would have required multinational corporations to inform and consult regularly with employees. The information to be given the employees was extensive and covered the entire operations of the corporation, including those outside of the EC (CEC 1980b). The storm which resulted from the proposal was, perhaps, the most severe of any which the EC has had over a proposed directive. The storm signaled the fact that the values and attitudes of the 1970s had fallen victim to the economic recession. Business values were in ascendancy and the course of policy making in the EC adjusted accordingly. Despite major changes suggested by the Parliament and accepted by the Commission, the Vredeling proposal lay dormant in the Council. The cycle of social legislation of the 1970s ended with the decade and did not revive again until the Social Dimension was added to the 1992 initiative. (No major piece of employment law was accepted between 1980 and 1986. A directive (80/987/EEC) passed in 1980 protects employees if their employer becomes insolvent [CEC 1980a].)

## THE SOCIAL CHARTER AND THE EUROPEAN COMPANY STATUTE

When Jacques Delors launched the social dimension in the fall of 1988, he reopened the controversy over industrial democracy by placing three measures for industrial democracy on his list of approximately eighty proposals for social legislation. Two of them were revivals from the past: the European Company Statute and the Vredeling proposal. The third was a European Charter of Social Rights. He promised to act on all three of those proposals in 1989 but was successful only in the case of the latter one.

In 1989, the proposed European Charter of Social Rights became the central issue in the general controversy over the addition of a social dimension to the 1992 initiative. Prime Minister Margaret Thatcher called the proposed charter Marxist interventionism. Commissioner Vasso Papandreou responded to the effect that, while the charter had little to do with Marxism, it had a lot to do with a democratic Europe. Consultants in the United States warned that it would destroy the effectiveness of the 1992 initiative, and European trade unionists stated that Europe would be social or it would not be. At issue was whether the EC should have a bill of rights for employees.

The procedure by which the EC obtained a Charter on Social Rights was unusual. Normally the Commission drafts proposals, the Parliament and the Economic and Social Committee consider them, and the Council votes to accept or reject them. Proposals are also normally in the form of a regulation, directive, or recommendation. In the case of the Charter, however, the procedure and the final outcome did not follow the norm. The idea of a charter of employee rights was considered in both the Council and the Commission as early as 1987, but no action was taken. Then in November 1988, the President of the Commission, Jacques Delors, in a little-used procedure, requested the Economic and Social Committee to "undertake a general appraisal of the possible components of a Community Charter of Basic Social Rights" (Economic and Social Committee 1989: 1). (The Economic and Social Committee is composed of three groups of representatives: employers, employees, and a mixed group composed primarily of agricultural and consumer interests in the twelve member states. It is a consultative body and issues opinions on proposals drafted by the Commission.) The Committee concluded that member states were already bound to respect many employee rights by existing laws and the Charter of Social Rights of the Council of Europe. The Committee also advised the Commission not to enact another international charter but rather to incorporate into the legal system of the EC those rights which required a supranational status. The Committee warned that the basic social guarantees of Europeans should not be relegated "to second place in the completion of the Single Market" (Economic and Social Committee 1989: 10). The Committee believed that some social rights were essential to the internal market.

The vote on the opinion in the Economic and Social Committee revealed some interesting schisms in European interest groups. The vote for the opinion was 135, with 22 opposed and 8 abstaining. The employee group, of course, supported the opinion. The other two groups split with most in support. The majority of those who opposed were British, further reflecting the continuing differences between British and continental employers. Continental employers are more accustomed to accommodating business practices to laws protecting employees and laws assuring worker participation. British opposition in the third group is more surprising because polls show that the British public supports a social charter.

The following month, the European Parliament passed a lengthy resolution on the social dimension in which it considered the question of basic rights for employees (EP 1989a). There was no ambiguity in the resolution. Parliament called on the Commission to give priority to the drafting of regulations and directives on fundamental social rights. It also called on the Council of Ministers for the "urgent adoption" of a directive for the application of fundamental social rights in all the member states of the Community.

The Commission was then under strong pressure to act. Jacques Delors had made many speeches to labor-union conferences promising that employees would not be left out of the new internal market. The members of the European Trade Union Confederation had acquiesced to the economic policies for the internal market, but their acceptance was conditional. They were now demanding social policies to form a "second pillar" to the 1992 initiative (European Trade Union Confederation 1988a). In May 1989, the Commission issued a preliminary draft for a social charter (CEC 1989c).

Seven months later the Council accepted the Community Charter of Fundamental Social Rights (CEC 1990g: 45–50). Only the British government opposed the document. The Charter represents an important step in the development of social policy in the EC. Social policy and human rights are now linked to give social policy a new importance. It is not just the handmaiden of economic policy.

In many respects, the Charter is an unusual document. It came into being by a procedure which circumvented the customary track for EC policy making. Neither the Parliament nor the Economic and Social Committee, the two institutions closest to employees, were officially consulted. The Parliament protested its exclusion. One member called the Parliament "the forgotten partner . . . but an obstinate one" (CEC 1990g: 14). The Commission was free to bypass the two institutions because the Charter is not in one of the forms covered by the treaty articles laying down the decision-making procedure. The method selected by the Commission traded democratic participation for speed. The seven-month history of the passage of the Charter must be a record for EC policy.

The Charter is in the form of a declaration, which is another unusual feature of the document. Declarations are not one of the five recognized forms for EC policy, so the status of the Charter as an EC policy is unclear. Is it merely a "motherhood" statement of principle without any true force, or does it have the dignity comparable to a national bill of rights? Vasso Papandreou, the commissioner responsible for the Charter, said that its basic function is "to offer a common perspective," but she also said that it does not impose a "social model" (CEC 1990g: 8). Jean-Pierre Soisson, the French Minister of Labor and the person responsible for the passage of the Charter in the Council, wrote, however, "This Charter establishes the existence of a European social model" (CEC 1990g: 11). Probably the significance of the Charter will depend on the success or failure of the EC in turning the rights contained in the Charter into EC laws.

The Charter is a concise document comprised of a preamble, twelve categories of rights, and a short passage on implementation. Two features of the preamble are important to note. One is that Article 100A of the Single European Act is listed among the relevant treaty articles authorizing the Charter. (EC laws or policies always mention the treaty provisions which empower the EC to act on the subject.) Some authorities have argued that this reference to Article 100A may constitute grounds for enacting measures contained in the Charter by a qualified majority vote in the Council. The other important feature of the preamble is the reference to the principle of subsidiarity which signifies that responsibility to implement the social rights "lies with the Member States or their constituent parts and, within the limits of its power, with the European Community." The principle provides an important constraint on the scope of EC authority.

The twelve categories of social rights are: 1) freedom of movement, 2) employment and remuneration, 3) improvement of living and working conditions, 4) social protection, 5) freedom of association and collective bargaining, 6) vocational training, 7) equal treatment for men and women, 8) information, consultation and participation for workers, 9) health protection and safety in the work place, 10) protection of children and adolescents, 11) protection of elderly persons, and 12) protection of disabled persons. Each category contains a list of relevant rights.

Many of the rights, such as the freedom of association and collective bargaining, are commonly found in comparable documents in Europe.

Others are rights which have long been known in EC law, such as the right to equal treatment for men and women. Few disputed those familiar rights. The ones which stirred controversy are ones which threaten to add to employers' costs or to add new constraints on the authority of employers. The right to workers in atypical work to benefit from an equitable reference wage is one of the controversial rights. Opposition predictably focuses on the provision for disclosure rights which evokes memories of the Vredeling proposal. Employers, who have long resisted international collective bargaining, also predictably oppose the provision for collective bargaining at the EC level.

The last section of the Charter once again invokes the principle of subsidiarity, but it also contains an invitation from the Council to the Commission to submit proposals for legal instruments to implement those rights which fall under the authority of the EC. The Commission is also instructed to compile an annual report on the application of the Charter by the member states and the EC.

The Commission prepared an action program to accompany the Charter (CEC 1989b). It is comparable to the 1974 social action program. It contains a work program consisting of forty-seven items. Each one is a specific proposal for an action which the Commission plans to take. Seventeen are for new directives, including eleven related to health and safety. The two most controversial of the remaining six are one for a directive on atypical work and the other on the health of pregnant women at work.

Several controversial proposals are for "community instruments." A community instrument may be a regulation, directive, recommendation, or opinion. The term is employed frequently when the Commission has not determined a form which is most politically acceptable. Persons close to the labor movement suspect the Commission of using the term to obscure the fact that the proposal will be introduced as a recommendation (which does not have the force of law) in order to appease employers and the British government. The most important and most controversial of the proposals for a community instrument is the one to require information and consultation in multinational firms. The proposal is a new version of the controversial Vredeling proposal of 1980. The remaining items in the action program are for reports or for recommendations.

The action program is an important document. Its scope is broad and ambitious. If the proposals contained in it are enacted, it will provide a significant layer of social policy at the supranational level of European law. The member states will be compelled to harmonize a good part of their employee law. The Commission appears to take its responsibility for the action program seriously and has already drafted proposals for many of the items promised in the action program and is working on others. The key obstacle, as always, is the voting process in the Council. The threat of a British veto is an ever-present consideration and casts a strong shadow of doubt on any prognosis of success for the action program.

In December 1990, the Commission proposed a new directive for worker participation (CEC 1990b). It fills a gap in the panorama of existing proposals on the subject. The Fifth Directive applies to national firms. The Vredeling proposal applies to both national and international firms but it does not stipulate a form for worker participation. The new proposal will apply to large firms operating in two or more member states. The terms of the proposal are simple and care is taken not to challenge the principle of subsidiarity. The initiative rests with the employees to open negotiations for a European works council. The structure and operation of the council is not determined by the directive but left to the negotiation between employers and employees. In the words of the Commission, the directive will be "simple, supple and flexible" (the Commission proposes a Directive on Information and Consultation of Employees 1990b).

The European Company Statute is the other major proposal relating to industrial democracy to be discussed in this chapter. While the history of the Charter is brief, the history of the Statute is long and complex, stretching over two decades. It was a focal point of the social 1970s and is a focal point of the new era of the social dimension, but it still has not been accepted.

The European Company Statute is not primarily a proposal for industrial democracy. It is rather a proposal to provide a legal form for a European company. Companies organize and operate according to the national law of the member state in which they are located. The Statute was proposed in 1970 in order to provide an option for companies in two or more member states to join together and create a European company operating under uniform EC law. Worker participation is one of the provisions contained in the proposal.

Two characteristics of the European Company Statute, as it was originally proposed, should be stressed. First, it was in the form of a regulation, which meant that it would be directly applicable and uniform anywhere in the EC. Second, it was optional. A company which met the criteria could choose to operate under it or continue to operate under the different national laws. National laws would continue to provide the legal framework for most enterprises. Both of those characteristics remained in the proposal when it was revised in 1975.

Opposition to the Statute always centered on the provision for worker participation. Both the German government and labor unions wanted a requirement for worker participation included in the law. They feared that otherwise firms would opt for the EC law in order to avoid national requirements for worker participation. The proposal offered European companies the choice of either the German or the Dutch model of worker participation. When that choice met opposition, the Commission unsuccessfully sought to find an acceptable form. The same problems which had delayed the Fifth Directive delayed the European Company Statute. Supporters of worker participation could not agree on a form, and many powerful interests opposed any form. Deadlock ensued and lasted until the proposal was withdrawn in 1982.

When the EC set to work to create the internal market, many realized that the market would need a European company. The proposal for a European Company Statute was revived. It was mentioned in the White Paper on Completing the Internal Market and in the Social Dimension. In 1988, the Commission issued a memorandum to take a sounding on the topic (CEC 1988f). The Commission argued that Europe needed transnational companies which would have substantial assets and would be independent of national laws in order to compete with American and Japanese enterprises. Response to the memorandum was positive. The following year, the Commission issued a new proposal for a European company law (CEC 1989q).

The Commission made a major change in the latest version of the proposal. The proposal now consists of two parts: one part in the form of a regulation (CEC 1989r) and the other in the form of a directive (CEC 1989q). The regulation contains the uniform provisions for a European company. The directive requires worker participation in European companies but provides various forms which are acceptable. The Commission hopes that the new strategy will at last enable the EC to achieve a European company law.

Although the proposed regulation does not include provisions for worker participation, it does state that worker participation is a mandatory part of a European company. Article 135 refers to the directive on worker participation and states that employees shall be involved in the European company. Article 136 adds the proviso that a European company can only be formed in a member state which has implemented the directive on worker participation. That proviso assures that the regulation and the directive are firmly connected.

The proposed directive on worker participation is based on Article 54 of the Treaty of Rome as amended by the Single European Act. The use of Article 54 is important because it would allow the Council to accept the directive by a qualified majority vote and thus increase the probability of enactment. Although the use of Article 54 is disputed, opponents must wait and challenge its use in a test case after the directive is implemented.

The directive must be implemented in law by the member states. Member states have the option of selecting one of the alternative forms of worker participation contained in the directive or incorporating all of them into national law and leaving the choice to be made by the employers and representatives of the employees in the companies concerned.

Three forms of worker participation are contained in the proposal. In one form, employee representatives participate on the board of the European company. Two options for selection of the representative are possible: the German model, in which employees select at least one-third of the members of the board, or the Dutch model, in which members of the board are co-opted, but employees have the right to object to the appointment of a particular candidate. In the second form, the employees of the European company shall select representatives to form a separate body with information rights. Management must provide information about the company every three months and more frequently if a major change is planned. The employee representatives are bound by rules of confidentiality as are representatives of the shareholders. The third model is the collective bargaining model in which employers and employees negotiate their own form of participation but which must involve information disclosure comparable to the other models. A labor union could represent the employees in that model. Employers and employees cannot agree to abrogate the requirement for participation. Share holding or profit sharing is permissible but is not adequate to meet the requirement for participation in a European company.

Critics of the directive raise serious questions regarding the equivalence of the three possible forms of participation. The first two forms place worker participation inside the firm in a legal sense. Management would owe fiduciary duties of good faith, loyalty, and full disclosure to the separate body. In contrast, management in the third form would not be bound by such legal obligations and, indeed, could be authorized by statute to withhold information that might be harmful to the interest of the firm. According to Paul Mortensen, the third model governs the rights of adversaries rather than common shareholders (Mortensen 1990).

Most observers believe that the European company proposal will be accepted. It was on the schedule of the Commission for 1990, but 1991 is more likely. The Commission has been ingenious in devising a form which provides for majority voting. The Commission has also been flexible in the search for an acceptable form for worker participation. The present proposal appears to offer enough benefits to business to make the participation requirement acceptable. If it is accepted, it will mark the first important victory for proponents of worker participation in the EC in two decades of effort and a significant advance in development of industrial democracy in the EC.

## CONCLUSION

The EC has taken a significant step toward the incorporation of industrial democracy into EC law. After an early flurry of interest, the topic had been dormant in the EC for more than a decade until revived in the 1980s under the impetus of the 1992 initiative. Industrial democracy, in the sense of basic social rights, was accepted by the EC in 1989. Industrial democracy, in the sense of worker participation, will most likely be accepted in the early 1990s.

The work of the EC in the area of industrial democracy builds on a broad base of acceptance and practice in the member states. The task was not easy, however. Important groups oppose incorporation of industrial democracy into EC law. In addition, diversity among the proponents of industrial democracy prevented a single form of worker participation from becoming the EC model.

Progress in achieving an EC policy on industrial democracy probably owes a great deal to the persistence of obscure Eurocrats in the Commission who kept the work alive through more than two decades and continued to search for acceptable forms. The Eurocrats were, no doubt, encouraged in their persistence by the European Trade Union Confederation. The Parliament also played an important role both in its formal capacity and its informal capacity as the champion of a people's Europe. The Economic and Social Committee, although a minor player, contributed especially to the Social Charter.

The politics of the Council regarding industrial democracy is fascinating. Governments try to manipulate the agenda of the Council so that popular measures are scheduled for a vote when they hold the presidency of the Council. (It rotates every six months.) The Socialist Spanish government tried to obtain acceptance of the Social Charter during its tenure. Prime Minister Gonzalez reportedly talked to Prime Minister Thatcher in an effort to win her support. He was not successful, and the

French made acceptance of the Charter the capstone of the European summit which marked the end of their presidency in December 1989.

The politics of voting in the Council is less colorful but more crucial than the politics of the presidency. The steady opposition of the British to social policies in the EC necessitated the drafting of both measures under consideration in this chapter in a special form so that they did not require a unanimous vote. For many years, the Commission sought to find compromises which would make measures acceptable to the British. Such compromises are less common today. Measures are drafted so that they have support of the other members. As noted earlier, conservative, northern European governments want EC social policies in order to force other countries to come up to the standard already prevailing in their countries. The more left-wing, southern European governments are committed to the measures on principle. The British are increasingly isolated. Political strategies which work when unanimous voting is required appear to be counterproductive when it is not.

One final point is worth raising for consideration. The EC is almost unique among current policy makers in Western Europe in its support for industrial democracy. The EC is customarily perceived as a remote and unwieldy bureaucracy with a "democratic deficit," but the study in this chapter shows the EC acting with flexibility to devise and adopt a policy with broad democratic appeal. Some have charged that the current social policies are due to the influence of French socialists, but the evidence does not support the charge. The apparent ability of the EC to enact policies with broad democratic appeal, despite its "democratic deficit," is an important point which will be raised again in later chapters.

# Chapter 8

# The Overlooked Parts of the Social Dimension: Health and Safety, Atypical Work, and the Social Fund

Industrial democracy and women's issues are the employment topics which attract public attention, but other aspects of the Social Dimension are equally significant. Health and safety is the area where the greatest advances have been made. The atypical work directive will provide protections for the growing number of employees holding such jobs. The Social Fund may hold the key to the successful creation of a free-labor market in the European Community. All three topics have been dealt with by the EC but take on new importance with the creation of the internal market.

## HEALTH AND SAFETY POLICY

The health and safety policy of the EC has made rapid progress since 1988, but few have noticed the development, and even fewer have sought to assess its significance. The relative obscurity of the topic probably results from several factors. The subject matter is technical, so it does not lend itself to public debate in the way subjects such as worker participation do. Health and safety is a "motherhood" issue. No one wants to oppose health and safety standards. In addition, health and safety proposals have a privileged position among social proposals. According to Article 118A of the Treaty of Rome as amended by the Single European Act, health and safety measures may be accepted by the Council with only a qualified majority vote. Health and safety proposals are thus accepted by the Council without the political fireworks which may accompany other measures. The final explanation for why the public is not aware results from the fact that the EC health and safety policy is drafted in the relative obscurity of Luxembourg rather than in the political hub of Brussels. Although most of the divisions of DG V (the Directorate General for Social Policy) are located in Brussels, the division concerned with health and safety policy is located in Luxembourg.

The history of EC involvement in health and safety policy traces to the treaty forming the European Coal and Steel Community (ECSC) which includes a provision for occupational health and safety in steel and coal industries. In those early days, the work of the ECSC consisted largely of compiling and disseminating information about safety problems in the mining industry, known for its high accident rate. When the Treaty of Rome went into effect six years later, it included Article 118, that empowers the Commission to promote closer cooperation among the member states in the social fields and specifically mentions prevention of occupational accidents and diseases as well as occupational hygiene. The EC did little to activate Article 118 over the next two decades. It passed two recommendations on health and safety in the 1960s and established an Advisory Committee on Safety, Hygiene, and Health Protection at Work in 1974.

The EC strengthened Article 118 in 1977, when it accepted a directive requiring uniform and clear safety signs in all work places. The following year, the EC accepted a directive limiting the exposure of workers to vinyl chloride monomer, a known carcinogen. That same year, the EC adopted an action program on health and safety, followed by several more directives also dealing with dangerous substances in the work place. The most famous of those directives is the 1983 directive establishing limits on asbestos dust. It contains a provision requiring employers to consult with workers on the use of asbestos. This little-noticed directive set an important precedent, as will be noted later. The second action-program on health and safety was accepted in 1984. It was the last significant development on the topic before the Single European Act.

The Commission outlined its plans for an ambitious, new program of health and safety in a report issued in 1987. The report states, "The Commission considers that the concept of the work place as formulated in Article 118A must not be limited to the health and safety of workers in its narrowest sense but must also encompass measures relating to ergonomics and the working environment" (CEC 1987a:11). The program includes five subjects: measures to protect workers' health, development of workers' safety, training and information policy, initiatives for small and medium firms and the development of social discussions. The document makes reference to the White Paper on Completing the Internal Market, which contains a number of proposed directives on health and safety among the measures necessary for the internal market. The document also notes the important relationship between standardization of equipment necessary for the internal market and the safety of workers. EC standards must incorporate a high level of protection for employees. The new program also contains proposals for fourteen new directives, but the more interesting parts of the document are the sections dealing with information, training, and discussion, because they reveal that the Commission is poised to expand its involvement in occupational health and safety. In the past, it studied and made laws. Now it will take on a more activist role. The Commission proposes to act to assure that employees are informed about and involved in health and safety issues in the work place. The new program inserts the philosophy of worker participation into occupational health and safety.

The report also contains a brief summary of the laws and the status of health and safety in the various member states along with a warning about the lack of reliability of the information. Most governments have not compiled a code of laws and regulations dealing with health and safety, so ascertaining the full range of protections is difficult. National statistics on occupational illnesses and accidents are also suspect. Reporting practices are not uniform; for example, France and Germany include accidents occurring on the way to and from work in their total for work-related accidents while other countries do not. The figures provided in the report show some differences which cast doubt on their validity; for example, the figures for persons killed in manufacturing indicate that Germany had the worst rate with 1,188 deaths. France was a distant second with only 409 (CEC 1987a: 35).

Although the figures probably include a high rate of error, they support the conclusion that the costs and suffering resulting from health and safety problems in the work place are unacceptable in the EC. The total cost is estimated to have been sixteen billion ECU in 1984 (1 ECU = US $.78 in 1984) (CEC 1987a: 7). That cost fell primarily on governments and their social security and health insurance programs.

The single most important directive which the EC adopted following the publication of the new health and safety program is the Council Directive of June 12, 1989, on introducing measures to encourage the improvement of the safety and health of workers (CEC 1989e: 1). The "framework directive," as it is known, establishes general principles for health and safety, which must be incorporated into national law by December 31, 1992. All subsequent EC directives for health and safety

will be based on the principles of the framework directive, and a list of
the topics to be covered by these directives is given in the annex of the
directive. The directive applies to almost every type of work place: public
or private, manufacturing or service.

The major portion of the directive deals with obligations of employers.
Many of the obligations are customary ones, such as the responsibility
for providing a safe work place. The difference between the many
provisions is not the subject but rather on the emphasis. Employers are
put on alert that health and safety concerns must become a high priority.
EC employers must be informed about new developments in the field
and adopt them in their work places. They are required to make
assessments of potential risk in their work place and to use experts on
the subject. They must respect the principles of ergonomics in all aspects
of work. Employers are also obligated to involve employees in their health
and safety programs. Such an obligation in the directive shows a strong
regard for industrial democracy. Employers must consult with employees
or their representatives when introducing new technologies. They must
designate one or more employees to have responsibilities for occupational
risks. Employers also have a broad responsibility for providing necessary
information to employees. Article 11 states, "Employers shall consult
workers and/or their representatives and allow them to take part in
discussions on all questions relating to safety and health at work." Finally
employers are required to assure that workers have adequate health and
safety training.

The directive has one article (Article 10) on employee obligations in
which employees are made responsible for doing what they can to assure
their own health and safety and that of their fellow employees. The
obligation of the employee does not affect the principle of the responsibility of the employer, however (Article 5).

The framework directive passed through the new decision-making
process of the EC, known as the cooperation procedure, in almost record
time. Parliament invited the Commission to propose a framework
directive on health and safety in February 1988. The next month the
Commission had issued a draft. Before the year ended, the Parliament
and the Economic and Social Committee had both considered it, and the
Commission issued a new version based on amendments proposed by the
Parliament. The Council took a common position on it in February 1989.
Following a second reading by the Parliament, the Commission further
changed it to include some eighteen amendments from the Parliament.
On June 12, 1989, the Council adopted the Directive.

The history of the directive is remarkable not only for its brevity but also for several other reasons. One is the important role played by the Parliament. The Parliament is becoming effective in forming social policy. In evidence of its effectiveness, the Council invited Lord Henry Plumb, the President of the Parliament, to speak to them about the directive, the first time such an invitation had been extended. The Parliament insisted on the provision for industrial democracy. Indeed, Parliament wanted the word "codetermination" used but settled for "balanced participation," which still carries the connotation of industrial democracy. The Commission redrafted the proposal two times on the basis of suggestions from the Parliament. Indeed, the Commission and the Parliament are allies and have a good working relationship on health and safety measures. The history of the directive is also remarkable for the small amount of lobbying which took place. A number of relevant actors have commented with surprise at the absence of lobbying. The European employers' association supports EC health and safety measures as long as they respect the principle of subsidiarity and do not harm flexibility (UNICE 1988b). Surprisingly, employers did not even organize to fight the provision for industrial democracy in the directive. The Confederation of British Industry did warn, however, that the framework directive introduces the social dimension through the back door via the majority vote (December Council Meeting 1989: 10-11).

When the framework directive is implemented, the requirement for "balanced participation" will probably cause the most controversy. A number of provisions will probably be tested in court. Two provisions in particular will probably cause some resistance. One is that employers will be obliged to assure that employers of workers from outside enterprises who are engaged in work in their work place receive relevant health and safety information. The practice of contracting out certain tasks is growing in the EC, so that provision is a new and important one for employers to note. The employers must also assure that workers temporarily in their work place have adequate training about health and safety risks. The second provision relates to the right of employees or their representatives to appeal to the government if they consider that the actions of the employer are inadequate to ensure safety and health at work.

By the summer of 1990, the Council had adopted five directives from the list in the annex of the framework directive. All of them deal with equipment used in the work place. One of these directives requires member states to adopt a regulation to govern the use of protective equipment for employees (CEC 1989g). It covers nine categories of equipment including hard hats, goggles, boots, and respirators. Another one of the directives deals with display screen equipment (CEC 1989h). Given the wide use of personal computers, the directive has implications for a vast number of work places. The directive set the highest level of protection for employees using that type of equipment in the world. Only Sweden has comparable legislation, but the Swedes reportedly believe that the EC directive goes beyond theirs. Employers must take steps to protect employees from wrist and back injuries associated with that type of work, and they must provide annual eye tests.

Work on health and safety measures continues in the Commission. Persons wanting to keep up to date on the topic should see *Janus*, the periodical on health and safety published by DG V. If the measures already adopted and those under consideration are implemented in work places in the EC, the standard of protection in the EC will exceed that found in the United States. Indeed, the International Labour Organization now perceives the EC as the example for the world (CEC 1989o: 8). The "if" is, of course, the crucial factor. The development of the EC policy has been so recent, and so rapid, that it is unlikely that member governments have fully grasped the extent of the obligations in implementing and enforcing the EC directives. The standards set by the EC are modeled on norms common in the wealthier members of the EC. Conditions greatly differ in countries such as Greece. Persons in the Commission defend this "leveling up," as they call it, on the grounds that the cost of prevention is less than the cost of treatment for occupational illnesses and accidents. Their perspective may differ from the perspective of employers, however, because the cost of prevention falls on the employers while the cost of treatment falls largely on national health insurance programs.

The Commission is beginning to widen the scope of topics included as health and safety, in order, perhaps, to qualify them for majority voting in the Council. The new topics proposed under the category of health and safety are more controversial than were the traditional topics. The publicity surrounding recent proposals has been much greater as well. In the summer of 1990, the Commission issued a proposed directive on working hours, which contains strict limits on night work and entitles all workers to a day of rest a week. Another proposed directive deals with the protection of pregnant women at work and includes a paid maternity leave. Opposition to both of these proposals is strong. Both would be defeated in the Council if subject to a unanimous vote, but the Commission believes that the measures are needed and that they are appropriately introduced under Article 118A.

## THE ATYPICAL WORK DIRECTIVE

The number of employees working in a job not covered by an open-ended, full-time employment contract is increasing throughout the EC. In 1990, fourteen million persons were engaged in part-time work in the EC, and ten million have temporary jobs. Over 20 percent of the work force in The Netherlands, the United Kingdom, and Denmark hold part-time jobs. Over 20 percent of employees in Spain are in temporary jobs. Although the percentages vary considerably among the member states, every one of them had an increasing proportion of their work force in both part-time and temporary work in 1988 compared to only five years earlier (CEC 1989g: 8).

In recent years, the EC has used the term atypical work to refer to a broad range of jobs not covered by the normal open-ended, full-time employment contract which traditionally covers an offer of employment in the EC. Atypical work occurs "where the job is not of indefinite duration or full time; or it is not performed on the company's premises; or it suggests the existence of two employers, or even the absence of any employer" (EFILWC 1988: 18). Persons in the Commission who study employment have reached the conclusion that the job market has undergone structural changes so that atypical jobs are a permanent and necessary feature of that market. Employers need a flexible work force in order to meet the challenge of global competition. They hire people on temporary contracts in order to meet a short-term increase in demand for their services or their product. They use subcontractors to perform tasks formerly performed by their own full-time employees. Teleworking and piece work are new and old variations of the practice of individuals performing work for an employer for a fee, but the work does not take place on the employer's premises. This latter form of work is sometimes referred to as "employment without an employer." Seasonal work and "on call" work are also considered forms of atypical work. In all forms of atypical work, the traditional tie between employer and employee is weakened, and employers have less of a direct responsibility for the persons performing that work.

According to a communiqué to the Commission from Vasso Papandreou, the commissioner responsible for social policy, people in atypical work often are subjected to subnormal working conditions (CEC 1990k). Persons who perform atypical work are most often from groups who lack the power to protect themselves and have few possibilities to move into regular, full-time employment. Minorities, unskilled women or youths, and the elderly comprise the majority of persons in atypical work. The national laws which relate to atypical work vary considerably among the member states, but none extends protection equal to that provided for regular, full-time employees. If the situation persists, the labor market in the EC risks an unhealthy segmentation into a core of privileged employees and a periphery of the unprivileged who have few opportunities to join the core. Where national protections are weak, labor costs for employers using employees in atypical work are cheaper than the labor costs for comparable employers in countries with higher protections or even in the same country for employers using regular, full-time employees. The situation, according to the Commission, gives an unacceptable comparative advantage to employers in countries with inadequate protections. It also compels employers to employ a larger proportion of their work force under terms other than regular, full-time contracts in order to remain competitive (CEC 1990k).

Part-time employment was the first form of atypical work to attract notice in the Commission. In 1981, the Commission proposed a directive which would have required extending to part-time workers the rules and provisions for full-time workers. The Commission rejected the possibility of special rules for part-time workers (CEC 1982b). The proposal was blocked in the Council by the British. The Commission tried for several years to find an acceptable compromise but finally withdrew the proposal.

The Commission continued to grapple with the question of part-time work and other forms of atypical work. It considered proposing a single directive covering all forms of atypical work, but such a proposal was unlikely to be adopted in the Council. In June, the Commission issued three related directives on atypical work (CEC 1990k). Each one is under a different provision of the Treaty of Rome reflecting the continuing effort of the Commission to gain Council approval for its social proposals. The decision was not easily reached in the Commission. One British Commissioner and both German Commissioners opposed the move.

The first proposed directive is to harmonize national laws relating to atypical work which distort competition. The relevant treaty article is Article 100 of the Treaty of Rome which requires unanimous consent in the Council. Under this directive, employers would have to inform their employees and consult with them about plans to use atypical employment. Employers would have to justify their decision. They would also have to provide equal access for such employees to training programs and other social services provided to regular employees. In addition, employees in atypical work would be counted along with regular, full-time employees to determine the threshold for compliance with national laws on worker participation. Most national laws on worker participation exclude firms with a small number of employees. Some employers are believed to have avoided the law in the past by using employees in atypical work and not including them in their employee total. The objective of these provisions is to assure that employers use atypical work only for valid economic reasons. Its objective is also to assure that employers in countries with weak protection for employees in atypical work do not have a comparative advantage over employers in countries with strong protection.

The second proposed directive is also designed to prevent distortion of competition among the member states, but it falls under Article 100A as modified by the Single European Act. Measures falling under that article are adopted in the Council by a qualified majority vote. The directive would require employers to pay full social contributions for all employees on atypical work contracts who work at least eight hours per week. In addition, employers should pay for other social benefits in proportion to the hours worked. The exclusion of employees in atypical work from social protections such as paid leave, severance pay and seniority pay, is considered unfair competition. Such employees are to be entitled to social protections in proportion to the total hours worked. The proposal also includes a limit of thirty-six months for temporary employment so that employers cannot keep employees as atypical workers indefinitely in order to avoid giving them the rights of permanent employees.

The third proposed directive is based on Article 118A and is designed to fit under the framework directive for health and safety discussed above. It assures that temporary employees have the necessary information and training in order to avoid health and safety risks. Employers are required to assess the risks in specific temporary jobs and to determine the qualifications necessary for employees to fill those jobs.

Many employers are disturbed by the proposed directives and believe that they will raise the cost of business in the EC with a resulting loss of global competitiveness. Certainly the implications of the directives are enormous, given the large number of employees in atypical work and the existing differences in national policies about them.

Passage of the three proposals promises to be difficult even after the adjustments made by the Commission. The Parliament joins the Commission in support of the goals of the proposal but has rejected the directive that requires a majority vote. Because the proposal does not fall under a provision of the treaty requiring the cooperation procedure, the rejection of the Parliament has no impact on the Council. It does signal, however, the dissatisfaction of many with the strategy of the Commission.

The proposals will face a more difficult time in the Council where the Germans have joined the British in opposition to proposals that will add a significant burden on many employers.

The Social Fund, like health and safety policy, has grown out of the treaty forming the European Coal and Steel Community. The fund was established to provide money to assist in retraining and relocating workers displaced by restructuring in the two industries covered by the treaty. When the Treaty of Rome was written, provisions for a social fund were included. Articles 123 to 128 set the objectives for the fund and the authority of the institutions in operating it. The purpose of the fund is to facilitate the employment of workers and to increase their geographic and occupational mobility in order to improve employment opportunities and raise the standard of living. The Single European Act provided for the Social Fund to be joined with the Regional Fund and the European Agricultural Guidance and Guarantee Fund into the Structural Funds and used to promote economic and social cohesion in the EC (Articles 130a through 130e). The Single European Act ordered the Commission to draft a comprehensive proposal to revise the operation and structure of the Structural Funds which must then be unanimously accepted by the Council after the Parliament and the Economic and Social Committee have considered it. The Social Fund is also discussed in the Social Dimension which states that the Structural Funds as a whole will have their resources doubled to reach 13.5 billion ECU (1 ECU=US $1.15 in 1990) by 1993 (CEC 1988k: 19).

Throughout most of its history, the Social Fund played a minor role in employment policies in the EC. The amount of money available was insignificant, averaging around 6 percent of the EC budget. The need was not great in the early days when the EC was small and its members prosperous. The fund took on new importance after 1972 when social policies became more prominent in the EC. Money was allocated from the fund to assist in retraining textile and agricultural workers. Training programs for handicapped workers were also assisted in the 1970s (CEC 1974a: 21-26). As unemployment grew in the EC, money from the Social Fund was used for programs to help young people enter the work force. After 1984, the fund's resources were targeted for programs for unemployed young persons and for employment assistance in the poorer regions. The addition of Greece, Portugal, and Spain in the 1980s increased the demand for aid. By the mid-1980s, the Social Fund needed reform. It was criticized for its inability to respond promptly and adequately to the demands on it, even though its funds had been increased to about 19 percent of the EC budget.

In 1988 the Council adopted a framework regulation to reform the structural funds as required by the Single European Act (CEC 1988h). The Council also adopted a regulation to reform the Social Fund as required by the framework directive (CEC 1988i). Henceforth, the Social Fund is to operate as part of an "integrated approach" with five objectives:

1. To develop the less developed regions of the EC.
2. To convert regions hit by industrial decline.
3. To combat long-term unemployment.
4. To facilitate the occupational integration of young people.
5. To modernize agricultural structures and develop rural areas.

The specific tasks of the Social Fund within these general programs are numbers three and four above. It is also to support measures for vocational training and for job creation. The Commission will also play a more activist role than it did when it was largely a passive donor to national projects. In the new partnership, the Commission will deal directly with local authorities, as well as the national governments, and will assure that projects are in accordance with the objectives of the Structural Funds. In December 1989 the Commission approved Community Support Frameworks (CSFs) with eight member states to define priorities for EC support for 1990-1992. The United Kingdom will be the largest recipient. Preference was given to transnational measures, measures to help modernize the production structure, including those in small firms and training in new technology (CEC 1990m: 191).

The allocations to the Social Fund have been increasing as have allocations to other parts of the Structural Funds, which are expected to reach a total amounting to about one-third of the EC budget by 1993. In 1989, the Social Fund spent 3.5 billion ECU (1 ECU=US $1.10 in 1989). Four billion is allocated for 1990, and the preliminary budget for 1991 allocates 4.3 billion (CEC 1990f).

If the plans for the Social Fund are fulfilled, it will play an important role in providing a qualified and mobile work force in the EC. In the past, it largely supplemented national programs, so its contribution was minimal. Some member countries, such as Germany, have excellent national programs. Others, such as the United Kingdom, have been less successful. The result has been a fragmented work force and areas with shortages of qualified persons and other areas with high unemployment among persons with outmoded skills. The prognosis for the success of the Social Fund in meeting its objectives depends, in part, on factors extraneous to the employment area. The EC budget continues to be constrained by high agricultural expenditures. The success of the Social Fund may well depend on a successful end to the long struggle to bring agricultural spending under control. Progress has been made, but agriculture still takes over half of the EC budget.

## CONCLUSION

The three parts of the Social Dimension discussed in this chapter probably have a greater relevance for the average employer or employee in the EC than do more well-known aspects such as the Social Charter. The importance of the health and safety proposals are obvious. The directives on atypical work will be good for many workers but costly for some employers. The new Social Fund should benefit both employers and employees.

All three topics existed in the EC before the Social Dimension, but all have been revised to meet new demands. The Commission has played the key role in devising the new strategies and in promoting the measures. The Commission has the support of both the Parliament and the Economic and Social Committee on these measures. The Parliament, in particular, is assuming the leadership in suggesting new policies and in publicizing social issues. Recently, for example, it has proposed that the Commission should draft a directive on child care, which would open the Structural Funds to be used for achieving more equality in access to public child-care facilities for working mothers (CREW 1990a: 3–5). The Council has also supported the proposals for health and safety and for the Social Fund. Opposition has been muted. The chances of success for two of the overlooked parts of the Social Dimension are quite good. The prognosis for the atypical work directives is much more negative.

The work of the EC on the health and safety directives and on the Social Fund fits into the area of technical, noncontroversial policies that have been deemed suitable for an entity in the process of integration. They constitute a "natural" spillover from the agreement to remove internal barriers to competition. Member states can perceive their utility. They are not issues on which it is easy to mount opposition. Their successful implementation will provide a basis for Europeans to regard the EC as having a direct relevance for them. According to one interest group, a shift in focus has already occurred and the EC is seen as the "engine" driving the process for improved health and safety standards in the member states (Environmental Resources Limited 1990: 11).

# Chapter 9

# Toward a Single Labor Market: The Free Movement of Employees

The free movement of workers and the freedom of establishment are two of the basic provisions of the Treaty of Rome. The founders of the European Community envisioned a true European labor market in which workers and people in the professions could move easily to areas which offer them the best economic opportunity. Despite some efforts by the EC to establish such a market, the goal remains elusive. Even experts in the EC admit to failing to achieve a goal set more than thirty years ago. "The European labor market is currently more of a concept than a reality," according to the authoritative *Employment in Europe* (CEC 1989k: 153). The EC continues to pursue the goal, however. Both the White Paper on Completing the Internal Market and the Social Dimension endorse a common labor market as an important objective.

As every tourist who visits Western Europe knows, many countries have a large number of foreign workers, but one must distinguish between migrants workers in the EC who come from another EC country and those who are citizens of non-EC countries. The free labor market foreseen in the Treaty of Rome consists only of the member states. Most EC policies, designed to facilitate the free movement of workers, apply only to citizens of an EC country. National laws and bilateral treaties between an EC country and a third country cover the situation for non-EC foreign workers.

Today, the foreign labor pool in the EC consists of about four million people, two million of whom are citizens of an EC member state (CEC 1989k: 153). The large migrant waves which characterized the postwar era ended in the 1970s. Most EC countries closed their doors to non-EC workers during the decade of recession. They could not close their doors to EC workers, but their movement stopped as well. Indeed, many foreign workers voluntarily returned to their homes in Italy or other southern European countries. The foreign workers who remained have become long-term residents accompanied by their families. They comprise the majority of foreign workers found in the member states today. Some indications exist for a new type of migrant workers far fewer in number and belonging to a different social stratum. This new type consists of white-collar or technical people who move about Europe as employees of transnational corporations. The traditional migrant workers need laws which protect their right to seek and to hold a job without discrimination. The new migrants need policies which assure respect for their qualifications throughout the EC.

EC policies have been directed toward the elimination of legal barriers to both geographical mobility and occupational mobility, but most experts today do not think that legal barriers are a major reason for the low level of intra-EC labor movement. Few expect that the successful implementation of EC proposals to remove legal barriers will significantly affect unemployment. The poor and the unemployed in the EC hesitate to move to another country in search of work for sociological rather than legal reasons. Language barriers, lack of skills, lack of housing and traditional family ties inhibit mobility probably more than legal barriers do. In addition, people in the EC are not compelled by the desperate conditions which created the migrant flows of the postwar era or those from Eastern Europe today (CEC 1988m). Sociological barriers are more difficult for the EC to eradicate, but the EC is beginning to consider them.

## FREE MOVEMENT OF LABOR

Through the years, the EC adopted several directives and regulations to provide for the free movement of workers. The two most important measures are the 1968 regulation on freedom of movement of workers within the Community (CEC 1968) and the 1976 action program for migrants and their families (CEC 1976). The objective of those measures is to assure that member governments do not discriminate against workers or their families who come from other EC countries.

In 1985, the EC adopted another action program for migrant workers, which broadened the responsibility of the EC for the free movement of workers. The migration policy at the European level is now to be considered as an integral part of the move towards European citizenship (CEC 1985a: 6). The Commission had studies made on sociological barriers to the free movement of labor. The new ideas did not translate into new proposals for action, however. Most of the proposals listed in the action program were ones already under consideration in the EC or were under consideration for more study. One proposal does concern European citizenship, but in language full of bureaucratic caution, it proposes "continuing to analyze the possibilities of wider recognition of political rights, both individual and collective, with regard to Community migrants" (p. 15).

When the EC launched the 1992 initiative, the free movement of labor was one of the basic principles. The White Paper on Completing the Internal Market states, in the introduction, that one of the aspects of the internal market is to ensure that people flow into the areas of greatest comparative advantage. According to the White Paper few barriers remain to the free movement of labor, but action is promised on cumbersome administrative procedures and on the problem of comparability of vocational qualifications.

At the present time, according to *A Guide to Working in a Europe without Frontiers*, a citizen of an EC country may travel to other EC countries in order seek employment and to work (Seche 1988). Even jobs in the public service (with a few exceptions) must be open equally to all applicants from EC countries. Workers and their family members are entitled to residence permits. (Action is underway to make work permits easier to obtain without necessarily being related to employment.) The employee may vote in work-place elections and participate in other work-related programs without discrimination. The person is covered by the host country's social security system. If the person becomes unemployed, he is entitled to unemployment compensation and his resident permit may not be revoked during the period covered by unemployment compensation. (The unemployment payments may stop, however, if the person leaves the country to seek work elsewhere.) From the legal perspective, citizens of an EC country enjoy access to employment in a single labor market comprised of the twelve member states. They even have the right to vote in local elections in three member states and will in all if a proposed directive is adopted (CEC 1989s).

The free movement of labor is dealt with again in the *Social Dimension of the Internal Market*. It states, "Social policy must, above all, contribute to the setting up of a 'single labor market' by doing away with the barriers which still restrict the effective exercise of two basic freedoms: the freedom of movement of persons and the freedom of establishment"

(CEC 1988k: 2–3). The thirteen proposals relating to free movement are modest in scope. Most are for regulations or directives to revise existing regulations and directives dealing with discriminatory national practices. In addition, the document contains a proposal to reform the European system for the international clearing of vacancies and applications, SEDOC, which informs workers about job opportunities throughout the EC. The employment exchanges of all the member countries would be linked. In the future, representatives of workers are to participate in managing and operating the system. The system is also to be expanded to contain information about living conditions and other matters needed by persons considering work in another country.

Given the commitment which the EC makes to the free movement of labor in all major policy pronouncements, the EC policy on the topic is rather limited. The primary objective has always been to remove legal barriers of member states which still impede the free movement of labor. The EC continues quite successfully to refine its measures to end legal barriers, but it hesitates to tackle more controversial problems, such as the difficulties arising from different social security systems or minimum-wage laws. Those difficult problems have been discussed but have been too controversial to become the subject of a formal proposal. The EC will probably undertake more controversial measures for the single labor market later, but not before the economic measures of the 1992 program are in place. From a realistic assessment, the EC has done about all it can do to provide for the free movement of labor. The legal barriers are largely gone; the sociological barriers are less amenable to EC policies.

## THE FREE MOVEMENT OF OCCUPATIONS

The free movement of occupations is directly related to the free movement of labor as well as the right of establishment. In order for persons to move freely for the purpose of work, their work qualifications must be accepted throughout the EC. The acceptance applies both to persons seeking employment and to persons with professional qualifications wanting to practice their professions in other countries in a self-employed capacity. Once the EC began to consider the problem of the comparability of job qualifications, it also inevitably had to consider the comparability of training and education in the different member states. The EC has made considerable progress in all aspects of the free movement of occupations.

In some member states of the EC, applicants for almost any type of job must have served an apprenticeship, must have a training certificate, or must have relevant work experience. Germany is a good example of a country where almost every type of job requires some form of formal preparation and gives to the holder of the job a recognized status. About 467 occupations in Germany have official apprenticeships (Lawrence 1980: 115). In addition, Germany is justly famous for its extensive vocational training program. Employees from high-level managers to skilled machinists to restaurant employees have their appropriate training and credentials. In other countries, formal preparation and certification for employment is much less common. This is especially true among the newer members of the EC, although the United Kingdom also has a weak system for job training. The national differences have been an important factor in impeding the movement of occupations.

The EC started work on the free movement of occupations in the 1960s. The EC adopted a number of directives, each of which dealt with a specific sector of work, such as wholesale trade or personal services. An objective of the directives is to assure that employers recognize work experience which applicants have acquired in other member states; for example, the 1982 directive for hairdressers assures that persons who have worked either as self-employed hairdressers or managers of hair-dressing establishments for a minimum time may have their qualifications recognized in other EC countries (CEC 1982a). Each directive has conditions suitable for the activity being liberalized. Some of the other sectors covered by comparable directives are for insurance agents and brokers, transport agents, and food and beverage workers.

For some other types of work, the EC has established standards for training or education suitable for the work involved. Once the standards are established, the EC adopts a directive which requires the member states to recognize the diplomas from other EC member states. Establishing standards and having them recognized is a slow and complex process. It has been used mainly for the health professions, including doctors and nurses. The directives also apply to lawyers and some architects.

Although the EC had adopted some sixty directives to facilitate the free movement of occupations, many occupations still were not covered by the time the EC began work on the 1992 program. The need for the free movement of occupations became more urgent. In order to speed the process, the EC adopted a new approach based on a general system of mutual recognition. A directive was adopted in 1988 to provide for the recognition of higher education diplomas awarded for occupations having a minimum training period of three years (CEC 1989i). It goes into force in 1991. A similar directive still pending is intended for the mutual recognition of diplomas for secondary-school courses or post-secondary-school courses of fewer than three years, which shows that the holder has the professional qualifications required to take up a regulated profession in the member state (CEC 1989f).

The new approach does not assure persons of automatic acceptance of their credentials. It only prevents the member states from automatically rejecting the foreign credentials. The state still has the right to consider the credentials case by case and may set conditions for their acceptance. The new approach supplements, but does not replace, the existing sectoral directives. Indeed, the EC probably will adopt more sectoral directives because they have the advantage of providing potential migrant employees *a priori* knowledge that their qualifications are acceptable throughout the EC. Experts working with the Commission and the EC Center for Vocational Training (CEDEFOP) have already established the comparability of vocational training qualifications for construction work, electrical and electronics skills, motor vehicle repair, and for the hotel and catering trade. Work on several other sectors is to be completed by 1992.

The quality of job training is a major concern in the EC for two reasons. Different levels of job training among the member states interferes with the free movement of occupations. The European Social Fund, discussed in Chapter 7, provides assistance to national programs to upgrade the work force. Inadequate job training harms the competitive position of EC firms and thus undermines one of the reasons for the 1992 initiative. The EC has consequently launched a number of programs to improve the quality of the work force in the entire Community. Those programs also have an international dimension, so that participants may increase their familiarity with other EC member states. The following list includes well-known programs but is not comprehensive:

1. The PETRA Program was established in 1989 after the heads of government of the member states agreed to the principle that all young persons should have the possibility of two years of vocational training following compulsory education. The objective is to establish an EC network of training initiatives which involve cooperation among participants in different member states and at both the national and local levels. The projects are to be innovative, using active learning methods and encouraging initiative among the participants.

2.  The Exchange of Young Workers' Program is designed to support international exchanges for work or training of persons ages 18 to 28. About 7,000 persons are involved in this program each year. A similar program exists for student exchanges for persons ages 15 to 25.

3.  The EUROTECNET Program is another recent program for young people. It is designed to improve the dissemination of innovations in vocational training for new technologies through demonstration projects and cooperation on research.

4.  The LINGUA Program started in 1990 after government leaders agreed that persons in the EC should know at least three EC languages. Support is given to improving the material available for language training and to diagnose the language needs of business. Many EC publications now have the text repeated in three parallel columns each in a different language.

5.  The COMETT Program is designed to encourage greater links between industries and universities in order to improve high-level training in the new technologies. It involves the transnational placement of students in higher education in enterprises.

6.  The ERASMUS Program is one of the largest and most successful programs, involving some 43,000 university students and 1,500 higher education institutions. Its initial budget for the years 1987–1989 was 85 million ECU (1 ECU=US $1.10 in 1989). The money is used for grants for exchanges of students and faculty and to encourage joint curriculum development among universities in different countries. It also funds the EC Course Transfer System (ECTS), a pilot project to promote the acceptance of transfer credits among universities so that students may circulate more freely among universities in different countries.

7.  TEMPUS is a pilot program adopted in May 1990 following the revolutionary developments in Eastern Europe. It will fund joint European projects which link universities or enterprises in Eastern Europe with partners in the EC to assist in the education and training in Eastern Europe, and to encourage exchanges among people involved in education and training in the EC and Eastern Europe.

Training and education programs play an important role in the EC today. The growth in the total number of programs as well as their funding over the last decade has been remarkable. The preliminary draft budget for 1991 lists a 32.7 percent increase in spending on education, vocational training, and youth policy. The total in 1990 was 150 million ECU (1 ECU=US $1.15 in 1990), so the new amount will still be quite modest. The programs are popular and reach many people who would otherwise have little reason to know about the existence of the EC. In promoting awareness of the EC then, the programs are successful, but the degree of the success of the program's primary objective, which is to help lay the basis for a better and more mobile EC work force, may not be apparent for a while.

## CONCLUSION

The free movement of labor is one of the basic principles of the EC. During the first two decades of operation, the EC sought to assure the free movement of labor by adopting regulations and directives requiring member states to end national policies which discriminated against employees from other EC member states. The EC has been quite successful in eradicating discriminatory national laws through the steady improvement of the relevant regulations and directives. The EC has considered proposals to link its work on the free movement of labor to the concept of a citizen's Europe, but it has not yet acted on the linkage.

By the 1980s, conditions had changed greatly from the period when the EC first addressed the issue of labor mobility. In the early period, large numbers of Europeans were on the move seeking work, and employers were experiencing labor shortages. In the 1980s, the inter-EC labor flows had almost ceased except for the movement of technicians and white-collar employees of transnational corporations. Unemployment was high, but the unemployed in the EC did not set off across national borders to seek work. Sociological and not legal barriers appeared to keep them home.

When the EC adopted the 1992 program, the question of labor mobility took on a new focus and a new importance. The emphasis shifted from the eradication of discriminatory national laws to an attack on the obstacles to the free movement of occupations. The EC was already at work attempting to set standards for specific occupations, but progress was too slow for the needs of the new internal market. A new approach based on mutual recognition of training was adopted to supplement the traditional approach to EC standards, which continues with renewed emphasis.

The attempt to provide for the free movement of occupations inevitably involved the EC in a concern with the quality of education and training in the member states. The latter part of the 1980s saw a rapid growth in EC programs for education and training. The programs aim to create a more competitive work force in the EC as well as a more uniform standard of education and training throughout the EC.

The politics surrounding the policies for the free labor market have been less explosive than the political struggles over industrial democracy but interesting nevertheless. The pursuit of the free-labor market has resulted in a "spillover effect" in which the EC has been drawn into the sphere of education policy, hitherto a sphere reserved for the member states.

The right of the EC to make policy for the free movement of labor is fairly unambiguous so long as it is limited to directives and regulations curtailing the right of member states to discriminate against employees in their country who are citizens of other member states. Article 48 of the Treaty of Rome grants the right of free movement of workers. Article 49 gives the Council the authority to make the necessary policies to establish that right through the cooperation procedure as determined by the Single European Act. The Council acts by a qualified majority. (The right of establishment which applies to self-employed persons is dealt with separately and is not discussed because employees are the topic here.) Article 57 gives the Council, acting under similar terms to those above, the authority for the mutual recognition of diplomas, certificates, and other evidence of formal qualifications. The difficulty which the EC has had with the free movement of occupations has resulted more from the complexity of the topic than from political disputes.

When the EC began to address issues relating to the quality of training, it broached a more contentious subject. In the 1970s, when social policy was in vogue, the EC started to deal with education but met strong resistance from some member governments. The Treaty of Rome has no provision granting the EC authority in the general area of education, so the EC progressed little until after the acceptance of the 1992 program. The topic of education was then linked to vocational education and the commitment to the creation of a competitive labor force. The education policy of the EC contributes to the creation of the internal market by eliminating barriers to the free movement of occupations.

Article 128 of the Treaty of Rome gives the Council the authority to act on proposals from the Commission and, after consulting with the Economic and Social Committee, to lay down principles for a common vocational policy. The Council may act on the basis of a majority vote under Article 128. Article 235 provides the EC with the power to act in order to obtain an objective given in the Treaty even though the power to do so is not explicitly provided in the Treaty. The implied powers provision has been linked with Article 128 to provide the basis for EC action in education.

Not surprisingly, the piecing together of an EC authority in education has fomented controversy. Political battles have marked the passage of each of the education and training programs listed above. The battle over the ERASMUS program almost resulted in its defeat. The majority of the members demanded that the program be proposed under Article 235 which requires unanimous consent in the Council and thus preserves the concept of national sovereignty. Even after the Commission accepted the idea that the program would be based on both Articles 128 and 235, large cuts had to be made in the budget of the program before it was accepted.

The popularity of the EC education and training programs has helped to alleviate the opposition to them. Participation in the programs has exceeded expectations. Members have agreed that the ERASMUS program will be based solely on Article 128. Both employers' associations and labor unions support the programs as well, so this most recent addition to the EC policy for the free movement of labor appears to be the most promising one for future developments.

The initial work of the EC on the free movement of labor is largely completed. The work on the free movement of occupations is well underway and targeted for completion by 1993. The creation of a competitive labor force or the "Europe of competencies," as it is called in the EC, is the new objective, and it has wide support.

*Chapter 10*

---

# The Meaning of the Social Dimension for the Future of European Integration

The new internal European market has a social dimension. The Commission of the European Community has kept its promise to build a social pillar to balance the economic pillar set in place by the White Paper on Completing the Internal Market. The immediate objective of the Social Dimension is to ensure that employees are not harmed by the creation of the internal market. Employees are to be protected from the short-term dislocations arising from economic changes. Employees are also promised that protections and rights currently provided for them by their national governments will not be undermined. The Social Dimension also has another purpose: to be a building block in the construction of a people's Europe in which Europeans feel a bonding to the EC comparable to a sense of nationalism.

Although the work on social policies is not finished, enough of the structure is in place to provide a basis for an assessment. Both the short- and long-term objectives of the Social Dimension need to be considered. The study of the Social Dimension also provides useful insights into the politics of the EC, so the assessment should include that topic as well. The assessment addresses three questions: 1) Does the Social Dimension provide a body of social policies comparable to the economic measures contained in the White Paper? 2) How has the creation of a social dimension affected the politics of the EC? and 3) What does the social dimension mean for European integration and a people's Europe?

The short answer to the first question is an obvious "no." The Social Dimension is designed to supplement the internal market, so the internal market is the first goal. The foreword of the Social Dimension states that it "is not in opposition to nor must it slow down the completion of the internal market" (CEC 1988k). The admission that the social dimension is not comparable to the internal market in terms of priority does not, however, prevent a more thoughtful consideration of the question.

Taken as a whole, the policies of the Social Dimension constitute a rather comprehensive set of protections and benefits for employees to supplement those already in existence in the member states. The policies are not designed to replace national policies, but rather to ensure that the effect of existing national rights and benefits is not eroded by the creation of the internal market. Some of the policies, such as the health and safety directives, provide specific and concrete protections for employees. Others, such as the Social Charter, establish European norms which should be respected by all participants. Together they constitute the bulwark against the negative effects of the internal market insofar as the Commission can foresee them and can keep them within the limits of the political realities of the time.

The assessment of the social dimension must be tempered by the knowledge that many of its aspects exist only in principle. Despite the battle fought for its adoption, the Social Charter cannot mandate any course of action for a national government or an employer. It is not an EC law. The principles contained in it may provide a beacon to guide EC policies, but they may not. The history of the EC is full of resolutions which were proclaimed, then disappeared with little discernible effect.

The assessment of the provisions for industrial democracy must also be much more modest than either their proponents or their opponents have predicted. It is one of the areas where the Commission has greatly diluted its original proposals in order to gain their adoption without enraging the opposition. The President of the Commission is reputed to have said that he does not want another Vredeling proposal (referring to the 1980 proposal which aroused intense hostility in business circles). The current proposals will not uniformly affect the EC because they provide so many options for worker participation. Their acceptance will legitimate the principle of industrial democracy in the EC but will not result in an EC form of worker participation. The failure to create such a form does not nullify the effect of the directives because they will require important changes in some member states. The more important consideration, however, is whether the directives will provide an opening wedge for future, more rigorous directives. As in the case of the Social Charter, no definitive answer is now possible. It will depend on the political climate in Western Europe in the 1990s.

The two parts of the Social Dimension which will have the most visible effect are the health and safety directives and the policies for the free movement of labor. Of the two, the former will have a much more immediate effect than the latter. Indeed, the health and safety policy of the EC is the most significant aspect of the social dimension. Not only has the EC succeeded in establishing uniform protections, it has done so at a high level. The EC will be in the forefront for the world in protecting the health and safety of employees. In addition, the directives provide worker participation rights which may prove as significant for employees as those provided by the much more famous and controversial proposals for industrial democracy.

The work of the EC to ensure the free movement of labor has led to important policies to provide for occupational mobility and for the upgrading of the qualifications of the work force in the EC. The EC now plays an important role in training and development. The role is only in its infancy and the funding is limited, but the foundation is laid and the support is strong, so further progress should be anticipated.

In assessing the Social Dimension as a whole, it does appear well designed to address the problems which may arise in the work force as a result of the creation of the internal market. The persons who drafted it seem to have considered the matter carefully and to have devised adequate measures, given the realities in which they operate. In general, those measures do not go beyond ones previously under consideration in the EC. The Social Dimension is not revolutionary and does not constitute a vast expansion of the authority of the EC. Its importance is less obvious. At a time when social policies are out of favor in the member states, the EC has emerged as their champion, albeit a modest one. The development of the Social Dimension ensures that the new internal market is not cast in the mold of Thatcherism, but rather remains more in the traditional European mold in which the ideology of the marketplace is tempered by a certain skepticism about unseen hands. The existence of the Social Dimension also serves to raise the interest of Europeans in the EC. Formerly the social policies of the EC lacked dramatic effect. Now they constitute a "social dimension" which, like "1992," serves to catch public attention the way a slogan or a logo does in a marketing campaign. The Social Dimension may then serve to encourage that emotional identity with the EC which must be a precursor to building European integration.

In regard to question two, the work on the social dimension has profoundly affected EC politics. It has mobilized certain political groups

and turned their focus on the EC. It has also provided a testing ground
for the flexibility of the decision-making process put in place by the SEA.
In addition, the work on the social dimension has led to a greater use of
corporatist decision making in the EC.

European labor unions are important actors in national politics in
Western Europe. They have also participated in the work of the EC. The
European Trade Union Confederation (ETUC) was formed in 1973 to
promote the interests of all democratic labor unions in Western Europe
in the EC. It has become one of the most important and most effective
of the many interest groups operating in Brussels. The leaders of the
ETUC were instrumental in promoting labor policies in the EC in the
1970s. They developed a good working relationship with DG V in the
Commission and with the Parliament. Most of the labor unions which
belonged to the ETUC remained more concerned with national issues
than with those in the EC, however.

The initial response of the ETUC to the 1992 initiative was one of
cautious acceptance. The ETUC supported the White Paper in the hope
that economic growth would lead to more jobs, better living standards,
and fewer regional disparities (ETUC 1988a: 44). The ETUC has
continued to support the creation of the internal market but only on the
condition that progress on the social dimension continues simultaneously.
They maintain a steady pressure on key points in the decision-making
structure of the EC to ensure the adoption of measures which employees
support.

The leaders of the ETUC believe that the President of the Commission
and the Commissioner for Social Affairs are sympathetic to employee
interests. They also count on a solid majority in the Parliament, so they
are now more optimistic about EC social policy than they were in the
1980s. The major barrier which they perceive is the provision requiring
unanimity for the adoption of social proposals in the Council. They can
count on a majority in the Council but not on unanimity.

Perhaps more interesting than the position of the ETUC is the response
of some of the national, labor-union confederations to current developments in the EC. The British Trade Union Congress (TUC) was always
a reluctant European, although it participated in the work of the ETUC,
so it was quite remarkable when the TUC welcomed Jacques Delors, a
Eurocrat and a Frenchman, as an honored guest at its 1988 annual
conference. A special report which the TUC issued on the 1992 initiative
explains its conversion (U.K. Trade Union Conference 1988). In part, it
is a case of my enemy's enemy is my friend, but it is also because the
leaders of the TUC now look to the EC for policies which will benefit

British employees. They hope that the EC will aid job creation in old industrial regions in the United Kingdom and stop the erosion of national employee protections, which has occurred under the Thatcher government.

The conversion of the TUC is the most dramatic example of the importance of the EC to labor unions in Western Europe. Most other members of the ETUC were not anti-EC, so their support represents only a change in intensity rather than a conversion. The leader of the French Force Ouvrière (FO), for example, argues that a unified Europe is the best hope for employees in France because it will enable European firms to become competitive in the global economy (Bergeron 1988: 10–11). Another member of the FO wrote the ringing line that Europe will be social or it will not be (Pe 1989: 19).

The importance which labor unions now give to the EC is bound to affect popular attitudes throughout the EC. About one-third of all employees in the EC belong to a labor union, so labor unions are a powerful communication link between public opinion and the EC. Labor union publications and newspapers close to labor unions carry the message into the homes of employees throughout the EC. Many labor unions are also closely linked to the major political parties supported by the working class. Those political parties are pro-EC as well, so the mobilization of public opinion is broadly organized.

Europeans strongly support the Social Dimension and the role of the EC in formulating social policy. Europeans responded positively to the first news about 1992, but support began to wane in the spring of 1988 as fears grew about possible negative consequences of the internal market. When Europeans were asked in 1988 if they regarded 1992 with hope or fear, 76 percent of those who responded answered positively, but Denmark, France, Britain, Greece, Luxembourg, and Germany all had over twenty percent who were rather or very fearful about 1992. In that same year, which was the year when the Social Dimension was introduced, 79 percent of persons polled in the EC supported a common social policy for the EC. Support was almost uniform among all the member states, with the exception of Denmark. People also responded positively when asked about specific measures included in the Social Dimension. Ninety-four percent supported a common EC health and safety policy. Even the more controversial proposal on industrial democracy evoked a positive response from 88 percent of persons polled (CEC 1988b: 19–25). In the fall of 1988, following information about the Social Dimension, public support for 1992 increased again and has remained high. A correlation cannot be proven between the relative popularity of

1992 and the Social Dimension, but belief that the two are connected is strong in Brussels.

Informal and formal measures all indicate that public awareness and interest in the EC has significantly increased recently. Polling information is substantiated by many observations. The media give more coverage than previously to EC affairs. The *Financial Times* probably leads in the extent and depth of coverage, but other national newspapers report EC news. Articles about Jacques Delors no longer require introductory information. He has become as familiar as many national politicians. Advertising campaigns vie for "European" appeal. The EC flag flies in all the member states. Even souvenir shops have begun to sell items marked with the EC logo. Whether or not the enthusiasm of the moment transforms into long-term public identity with the EC probably depends on the success of the EC in developing policies which directly relate to Europeans and the absence of another recession.

The politics of the social dimension has also affected policy making in the EC in two important ways: It has helped to democratize it, and it has made it more flexible. The Parliament has been an assertive participant in every aspect relating to the social dimension. The Council can no longer ignore the Parliament, in part, because of the authority given Parliament by the SEA, but also because Parliament can now speak with more authority as the democratic voice in the EC. When the people are interested and the press keeps them informed, the Parliament can bring great pressure to bear on the Council. Of the 518 members of the European Parliament who were elected in 1989, the Socialists form the largest group with 182 members. The next largest group is the European People's party, which is a grouping of Christian Democrats, with 106 members. The Socialists are close to the labor unions but many Christian Democrats are, too. In addition, the President of the Parliament is a Socialist. When the Parliament now threatens to withhold action on measures for the internal market unless social measures are adopted, the threat carries meaning.

The Parliament has clashed with the Commission and the Council over social measures. The clash has helped to push the Commission to more strongly promote social measures, most notably the pressure has encouraged the Commission to devise means that will ensure the passage of social measures in the Council, as will be discussed below. Pressure from the Parliament also helps to keep a balance in the Commission between those who want to push ahead on the internal market and avoid confrontation with business groups and those who believe that the social dimension must progress equally with measures for the internal market.

Jacques Delors has assured the Parliament on many occasions that the Commission puts a high priority on social policy.

Socialists either participate in the government or form the major opposition party in every country in the EC. No cabinet minister from a national government participating in a meeting of the Council can ignore the political implications of his/her vote. Politicians from across the political spectrum have supported social proposals when they come before the Council for a vote. Only members from the British government have consistently opposed social policy. If the new British government is more pragmatic than the Thatcher government, then the way will be open for more bargaining in the formation of social policy, as already occurs for measures concerning the internal market. Members of the Council are first and primarily politicians in their national governments. They are responsive to political currents at home.

The Commission has used the provisions of the SEA in order to avoid the political conflicts inherent in the social dimension which the *Economist* once called "the passionate dimension" (The Passionate Dimension 1989: 56). One of the ways it has tested the limits of the SEA is by redrafting social measures, such as the proposals on maternity leave and atypical work, so that they fall under an article of the treaty which requires only a qualified majority vote for adoption by the Council. Another way is to invoke the principle of subsidiarity in order to encourage the social partners to play a greater role in social policy formation.

The most important example of involvement of the partners in social policy is the Val Duchese process. The SEA states in Article 22, which amends Article 118 of the Treaty of Rome, "The Commission shall endeavor to develop the dialogue between management and labor at the European level which could, if the two sides consider it desirable, lead to relations based on agreement." The Commission had already started a social dialogue with the social partners prior to the SEA. Experience with the social action program had revealed the need for an ongoing dialogue with employers and employee representatives. In 1985, the Commission called an important meeting with representatives from labor and employers in which the Commission charged the social partners with the responsibility of developing joint relations at the EC level. The Council confirmed its support for the social dialogue at the 1988 summit in Hanover.

The Val Duchese process has had limited success. Both employers and labor have reservations about the process. Employers fear that it will become a stepping stone to European-level collective bargaining. The process faltered after its initial period but was revitalized in 1990. The participants have discussed, and in some cases reached, a common position on a means to stimulate the growth of employment, the implementation of new technology, and various topics related to training and development.

The Val Duchese process is only one example of many arenas where the social partners are involved in policy making in the EC. The formal decision-making process disguises the fact that a strong element of corporatism is found in the process. The social partners participate in the work of the Economic and Social Committee which has the right to be consulted and to issue an opinion on many proposals for directives. The partners also participate in a number of standing committees inside the EC which are regularly consulted about social issues. The Standing Committee on Employment traces back to 1970 when labor unions demanded a permanent body inside the EC to deal with growing concerns about unemployment. It has an important role in determining programs to be included in the Social Fund. In addition, seven advisory committees exist. Two of the most important are the Advisory Committee on Safety, Hygiene, and Health Protection, and the Advisory Committee on Equal Opportunities for Women and Men. A number of sectoral committees also exist to bring together relevant representatives from labor and employers for sectors such as the maritime sector.

Whenever the experts in the Commission start to draft a proposal, they have interested parties readily available for consultation in the appropriate committees as well as in the numerous pressure groups in Brussels. The current Commission, under Jacques Delors, has encouraged such corporatism. The process is facilitated by the small number of people on the Commission who draft proposals on a particular subject and who rework them as needed. Perhaps three to five persons will be responsible for all the work issuing from the Commission on a single topic, such as health in the work place. There is little turnover among personnel in divisions such as DG V. The persons working there are experts on specific topics, such as labor policy, health policy, or the issues concerning women. They, not surprisingly, believe in the value of what they are doing. They are generally accessible to interested persons on the standing committees or interest groups. In such behind-the-scenes communicating, much of the work of the EC is carried on. The commissioners are generalists who must depend on their civil servants. The members of the Council are national politicians who consider only the finished draft of a proposal. Members of Parliament have neither the staff nor the authority to draft policy. Obscure Eurocrats, working closely with interested parties, produce the proposals which comprise the Social Dimension.

The answer to the third question: "What does the social dimension mean for European integration?" has largely been answered. The social dimension is the most important building block to date in the construction of a people's Europe. The social dimension has served to mobilize popular involvement in the EC, which will lead to greater identification with it as well. The process of mobilization and involvement is only in the early stages, however, and could still be reversed if Europeans become disillusioned with the outcome of the current program.

The crisis in Eastern Europe raises serious questions about continuing progress on EC social policy. The threat of waves of Eastern Europeans swamping the job markets of the EC is a major concern of many Europeans. The initial response of the EC has been twofold. It has started aid programs which are designed to create jobs in Eastern Europe and keep East Europeans at home. It has also hastened the process of integration in order to minimize the destabilizing impact of the crisis on members of the EC. Leaders from countries such as Spain support this effort because they fear that the crisis will deflect the funds and programs which they believe will come to them in the course of creating the internal market. European labor unions are also working to support the policies of the EC in Eastern Europe because they know that their influence on the EC will be lessened if the ranks of the unemployed in the EC is enlarged by a massive influx of job seekers from Eastern Europe.

The Social Dimension has provided the EC with a comprehensive social policy and resulted in a limited transfer of responsibility for social well-being from the member states to the EC. The authority of the EC is limited in regard to some of the provisions contained in the Social Dimension by their lack of a strong legal basis, and the effect of the Social Dimension on the actual practices of enterprises operating inside the EC will be felt only gradually and not uniformly as the directives are implemented, with variations, into national law.

This study concludes with an observation raised in the course of the study which invites speculation. Much has been said about the democratic deficit in the EC. Persons who believe in democracy become uneasy as they watch the EC expand. The formal procedure for policy making in the EC does not accord with normal democratic standards, but the development of the social policy shows the EC creating democratic policies by less than democratic means (democratic policies in the sense that the policies have approval ratings as measured in polls of at least 70 percent). The creation is all the more remarkable in a time when the democratic governments who belong to the EC are unable to enact such policies despite broad popular support. The paradox of the EC and its policies invites further consideration.

During the course of this study it has been found that the old tools provided by the functionalists are useful for understanding the process of making EC social policy. The social dimension is a spillover effect of 1992. The acceptance of an important initiative for economic policy brought the need for social measures to ameliorate the impact of the economic policy and also to encourage broad public support for the efforts of the EC. According to theorists on the EC, the transfer of authority—even in the limited measure indicated in this study—for welfare measures from member states to the EC is an indicator of integration (Taylor 1983: 196).

The politics of EC social policy exhibit the hallmarks of functionalism. The development of the policy has been incremental and cautious in order to avoid political conflict. Much of the work has been on measures that are technical and where the need for EC action is broadly perceived. Not surprisingly, the greatest progress has been on health and safety measures which are not perceived as political and which depend on the work of experts. The initiative for the social policy has been supplied primarily by the Commission acting as an institutional interest group as defined by functionalists (Caporaso 1974: 95). The existence of the proposals has, in turn, strengthened EC interest groups such as the ETUC. According to functionalists, the development of interest groups at the EC level is significant for the process of integration. As shown in the study, the strengthening of the interest groups was the result of both push and pull factors. Interests at the national level were pushed to turn to the EC by the unreceptive national climate. They were pulled to the EC by the initiatives arising in the Commission. The result is that the EC is now perceived as a legitimate arena for a wide range of policies and the EC has become a cognitive fact for Europeans. The validity of the assertion is attested to by the calling of a new intergovernmental conference to negotiate a treaty for further political integration. The broadening of the scope of EC policy has led the spillover effect to reform the policy-making process in the EC.

*Appendix*

# Charts of Employment Statistics

**LEGEND FOR CHARTS**

| | | |
|---|---|---|
| NL | = | The Netherlands |
| UK | = | United Kingdom |
| DK | = | Denmark |
| F | = | France |
| B | = | Belgium |
| IRL | = | Ireland |
| L | = | Luxembourg |
| P | = | Portugal |
| I | = | Italy |
| GR | = | Greece |
| D | = | Germany |
| E | = | Spain |

All countries do not appear on all charts since different countries entered the community at different times.

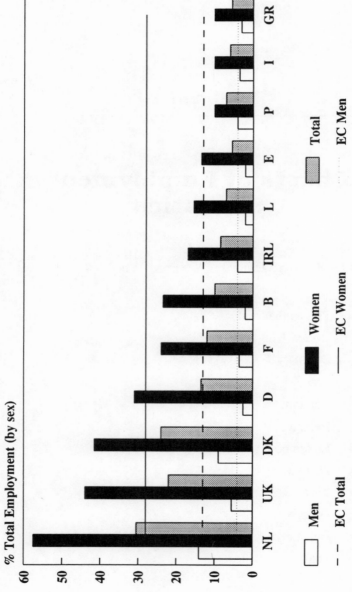

Part-Time Employment as a Share of Total Employment in the Member States, 1988

% Total Employment (by sex)

Men   Women   Total

EC Total   EC Women   EC Men

Source:   Commission of the European Communities. 1990. *Employment in Europe, 1990*. Brussels: Author.

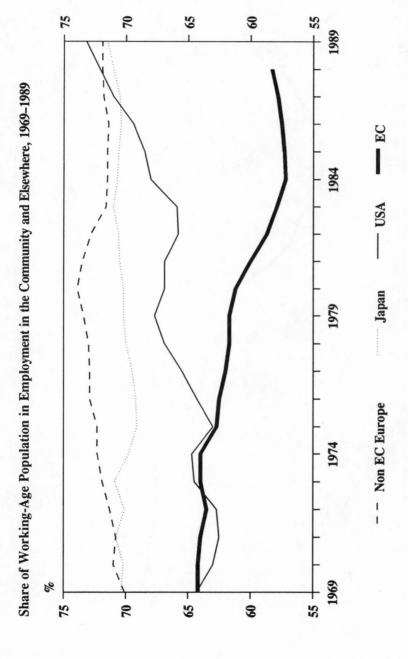

**Share of Working-Age Population in Employment in the Community and Elsewhere, 1969–1989**

– – Non EC Europe ........ Japan —— USA ━━ EC

**Source: Commission of the European Communities. 1990.** *Employment in Europe, 1990.* **Brussels: Author.**

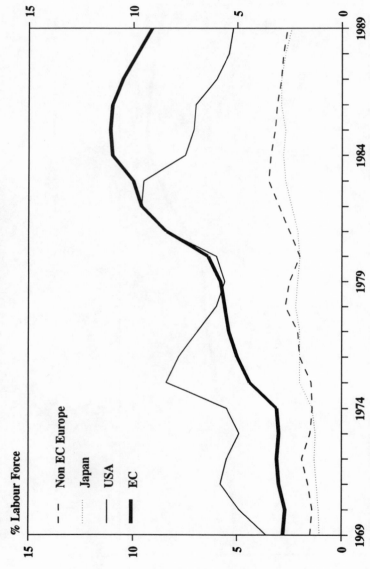

Unemployment Rates in the Community and Elsewhere, 1969–1989

% Labour Force

- – Non EC Europe
...... Japan
— USA
▬▬ EC

Source: Commission of the European Communities. 1990. *Employment in Europe, 1990.* Brussels: Author.

134

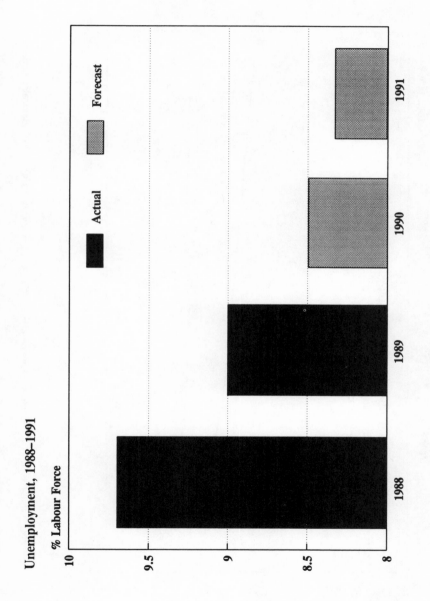

Unemployment, 1988–1991

% Labour Force

Actual

Forecast

10

9.5

9

8.5

8

1988

1989

1990

1991

Source: Commission of the European Communities. 1990. *Employment in Europe, 1990*. Brussels: Author.

Real Wages, Labour Productivity, and Capital Stock per Person Employed in the Community, 1970–1989

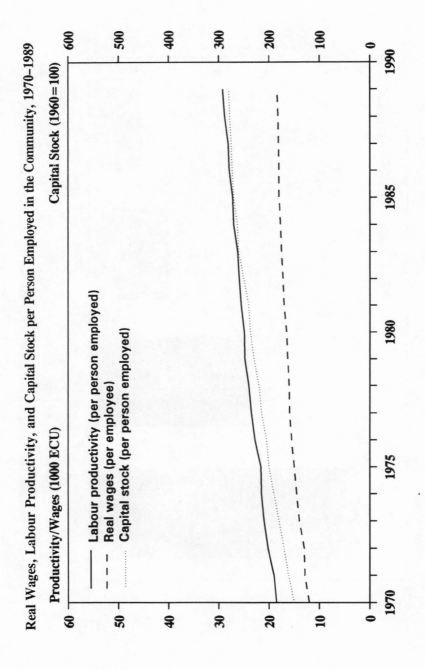

Source: Commission of the European Communities. 1990. *Employment in Europe, 1990.* Brussels: Author.

# Changes in Hourly Earnings of Manual Workers in Manfacturing in the Member States, 1979–1988

## Average Annual % Change

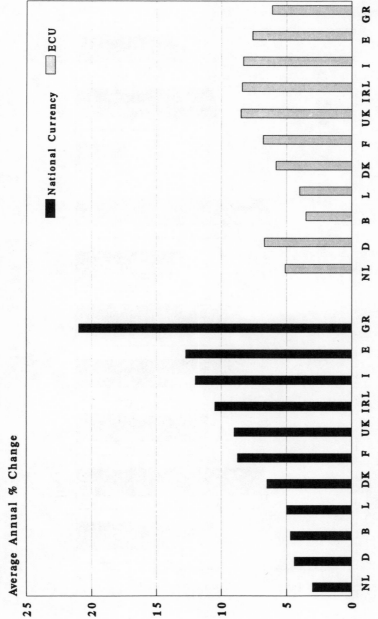

Source: Commission of the European Communities. 1990. *Employment in Europe, 1990*. Brussels: Author.

**Hourly Earnings of Women as a Percent of Male Earnings in Manufacturing in the Member States, 1973, 1979, 1988**

% Male Earnings

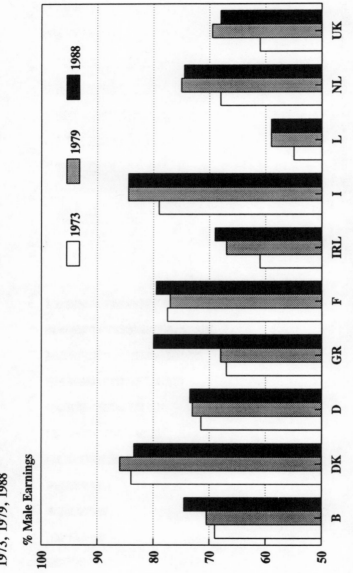

DK & IRL 1975/1979/1988
I & NL 1973/1979/1985

Source:  Commission of the European Communities. 1990. *Employment in Europe, 1990.* Brussels: Author.

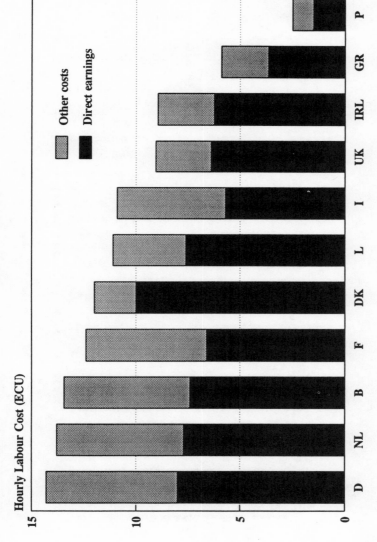

Structure of Hourly Labour Costs in the Member States, 1984

Hourly Labour Cost (ECU)

Other costs

Direct earnings

D  NL  B  F  DK  L  I  UK  IRL  GR  P

Source: Commission of the European Communities. 1990. *Employment in Europe, 1990*. Brussels: Author.

# Compensation per Employee in ECU by Sector in the Member States, 1986

## 1000 ECU per employee

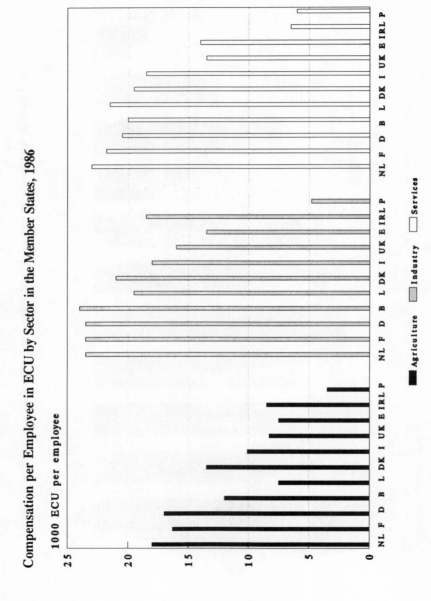

Source: Commission of the European Communities. 1990. *Employment in Europe, 1990*. Brussels: Author.

# Unit Labour Costs by Sector in the Member States, 1986

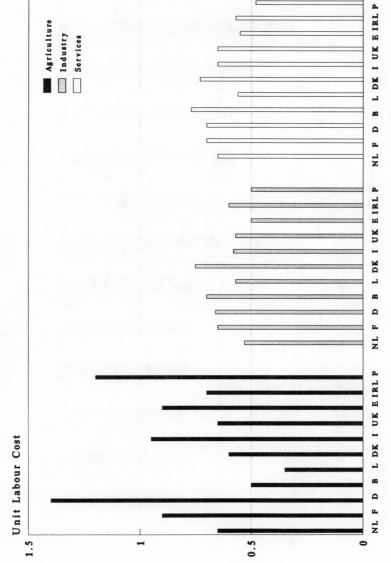

Source: Commission of the European Communities. 1990. *Employment in Europe, 1990.* Brussels: Author.

# Activity Rates of Women in the Member States, 1979 and 1988

Activity rate (%)

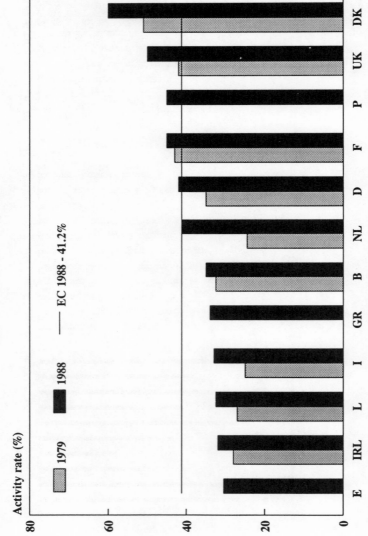

EC 1988 - 41.2%

1988

1979

E   IRL   L   I   GR   B   NL   D   F   P   UK   DK

80   60   40   20   0

Source: Commission of the European Communities. 1990. *Employment in Europe, 1990*. Brussels: Author.

Share of Employees Working Under Temporary Contracts in the Member States, 1988

% Employees

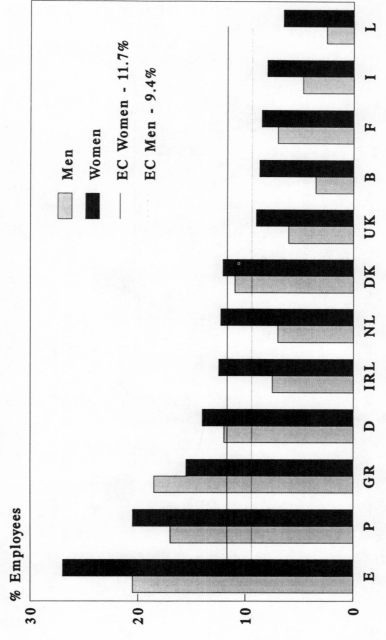

Source: Commission of the European Communities. 1990. *Employment in Europe, 1990.* Brussels: Author.

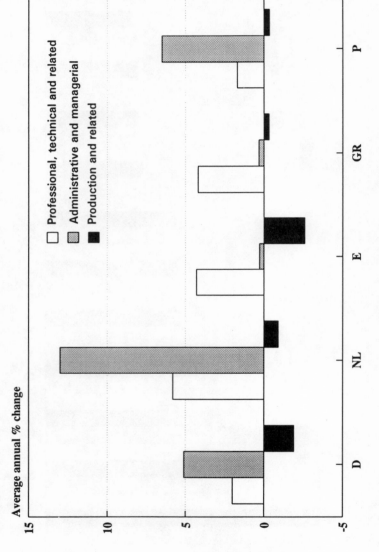

Occupation Changes in Five Member States, 1981–1987

Average annual % change

Professional, technical and related

Administrative and managerial

Production and related

D       NL       E       GR       P

D = 1980-86  E = 1976-86  P = 1983-87

Source:   Commission of the European Communities. 1990. *Employment in Europe, 1990.* Brussels: Author.

144

Installed Base (office and home) of Personal Computers in the Community, 1983–1988

Thousands of units

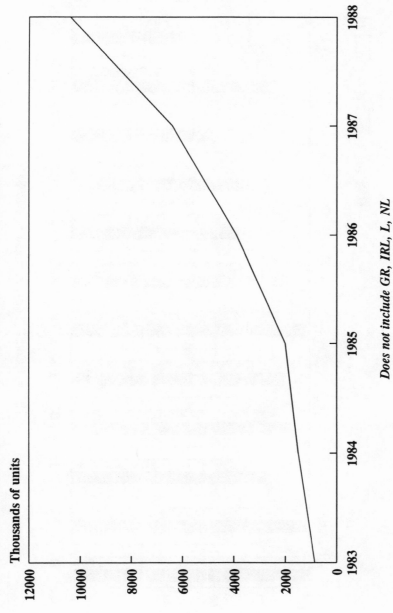

*Does not include GR, IRL, L, NL*

Source:   Commission of the European Communities. 1990. *Employment in Europe, 1990.* Brussels: Author.

145

**Sixteen to Eighteen Year Olds Participating in Education or Training in the Member States, 1985/86**

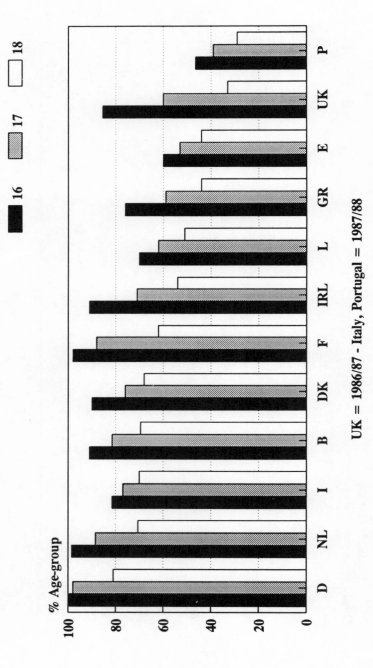

UK = 1986/87 - Italy, Portugal = 1987/88

Source:   Commission of the European Communities. 1990. *Employment in Europe, 1990.* Brussels: Author.

**Proportion of Young People Receiving Post-Compulsory Education or Training by the Age of Twenty-Four in Some Member States**

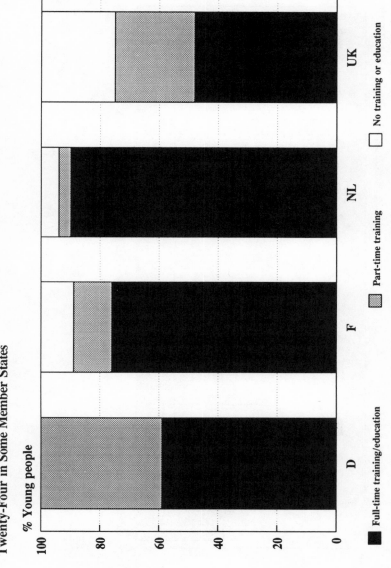

% Young people

■ Full-time training/education   ▨ Part-time training   □ No training or education

Source: Commission of the European Communities. 1990. *Employment in Europe, 1990.* Brussels: Author.

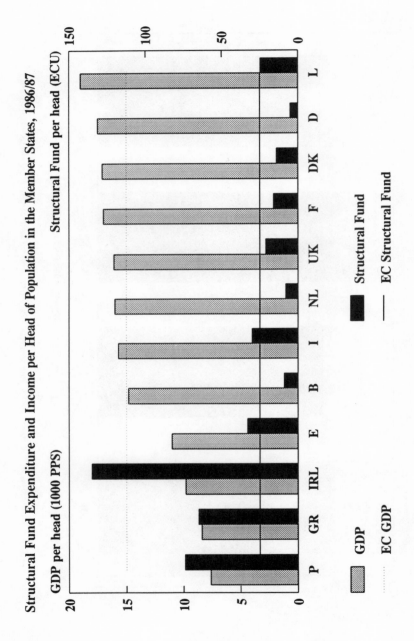

Structural Fund Expenditure and Income per Head of Population in the Member States, 1986/87

GDP per head (1000 PPS)

Structural Fund per head (ECU)

GDP

Structural Fund

EC GDP

EC Structural Fund

Source: Commission of the European Communities. 1990. *Employment in Europe, 1990*. Brussels: Author.

# Bibliography

Bergeron, A.
1988    L'Europe. *Force Ouvrière Hebdo* [official organ of the French CGT-FO] (September 14).

Bieber, R., R. Dehouse, J. Pinder, and J.H.H. Weiler, eds.
1988    *1992: One European market.* Baden-Baden: Womos Verlagessellschaft.

Braun, H., H. Laumer, W. Leibfritz, and H. C. Sherman, eds.
1983    *The European economy in the 1980s.* London: Gower.

Brewster, C., and P. Teague.
1989    *The European community social policy.* London: Institute of Personnel Management.

Budd, S. A., and A. Jones.
1989    *The European Community: A guide to the maze.* 3d. ed. London: Kogan Page.

Calingaert, M.
1988    *The 1992 challenge from Europe.* Washington: National Planning Association.

Caporaso, J. A.
1974    *The structure and function of European integration.* Pacific Palisades, CA: Goodyear Publishing Co.

CEC (Commission of the European Communities)
1968    *Regulation as regards the free movement of employed persons,* 1612/68. Brussels: Commission of the European Communities.

1974a   *Report on the development of the social situation in the Community in 1973.* Brussels: Commission of the European Communities.

1974b    Social action programme. *Bulletin of the European Community* Supplement 2.

1975a    *Directive 75/129/EEC on the approximation of the laws of the member states relating to collective redundancies* (February 17).

1975b    Employee participation and company structure in the European Community. *Bulletin of the European Communities* Supplement 8.

1976     *Official Journal*, C 34, 14.2.1976. Brussels: Commission of the European Communities.

1977     *Directive 77/187/EEC on the approximation of the laws of the member states relating to the safeguarding of employee's rights in the event of transfers of undertakings, businesses or parts of business* (February 14).

1980a    *Directive 80/987/EEC on the approximation of the laws of the member states relating to the protection of employees in the event of the insolvency of their employer.* Brussels: Commission of the European Communities (October 20).

1980b    *Proposal for a directive on procedures for informing and consulting the employees of undertakings with complex structures, in particular transnational undertakings* COM (80) 423 Final. Brussels: Commission of the European Communities.

1981     *A new community action programme on the promotion of equal opportunities for women* COM (81) 758. Brussels: Commission of the European Communities.

1982a    *Directive 82/489/EEC  on laying down measures to facilitate the effective exercise of the right of establishment and freedom to provide services in hair dressing.* Brussels: Commission of the European Communities (July 19).

1982b    *Directive on voluntary, part-time work* COM (82) 830 Final. Brussels: Commission of the European Communities.

1983     Community law and women. *Women of Europe* Supplement 12.

1984a    *Council recommendation on the promotion of positive action for women*, 84/635/EEC. Brussels: Commission of the European Communities (December 13).

1984b    *Progress report on the implementation of the new community action programme on the promotion of equal opportunities for women* COM (83) 781 Final. Brussels: Commission of the European Communities.

1985a    Guidelines for a Community policy on migrants. *Bulletin of the European Community* Supplement 9.

1985b    White Paper on completing the internal market COM (85) 310 Final. White Paper from the Commission to the European Council. Brussels: Commission of the European Communities.

1986a    *Directive 86/613/EEC on the application of the principle of equal treatment between men and women engaged in an activity, including agriculture, in a self-employed capacity, and on the protection of self-employed women during pregnancy and motherhood.* Brussels: Commission of the European Communities (December 11).

1986b    *Women of Europe* Supplement 23. The Women's Information Service in DG X.

1987a    *Commission communication on its programme concerning safety, hygiene and health at work* COM (87) 520 Final. Brussels: Commission of the European Communities.

1987b    France. *The Basic Information Reports.* Maastricht: European Centre for Work and Society.

1988a    Annual economic report, 1988-89: Preparing for 1992. *European Economy*, 38.

1988b    *Eurobarometer*, No. 30 (December).

1988c    Europe in figures. *EUROSTAT Series.* Luxembourg: Office of Official Publications.

1988d    *Framework regulation on the reform of the structural funds* (EEC) 2052/88, O.J. L 185 (July 15).

1988e    *Implementing regulation on the European social fund* (EEC) 4255/88 O.J. L 374 (December 31).

1988f    Memorandum on the statute for the European Company, COM (88) 320 Final. *Bulletin of the EC* Supplement 388. Brussels: Commission of the European Communities.

1988g    *Report on social development.* Brussels: Commission of the European Communities.

1988h    *Regulation 2052/88 on the reform of the structural funds.* Brussels: Commission of the European Communities.

1988i    *Regulation 4255/88 on the European Social Fund.* Brussels: Commission of the European Communities.

1988j    Report on the implementation of the Council resolution on action to combat female unemployment. *Bulletin of the European Community*, 12.

1988k    *Social dimension of the internal market* SEC (88) 1148 Final. Brussels: Commission of the European Communities.

1988l    *The dignity of women at work.* A report on the problem of sexual harassment in the member states of the European Communities. Luxembourg: Office of Official Publications.

1988m    The social dimension of the internal market: Interim report of the interdepartmental working party. *Social Europe*, Special Edition.

1989a    Basic statistics of the Communities. 26th ed. *EUROSTAT Series.* Luxembourg: Office of Official Publications.

1989b    *Communication from the Commission concerning its action programme relating to the implementation of the community charter of basic social rights for workers* COM (89) 568 Final. Brussels: Commission of the European Communities.

1989c    *Community charter of fundamental social rights* COM (89) 248 Final. Brussels: Commission of the European Communities.

1989d    *Comparative study on rules governing working conditions in the member states* SEC (89) 1137. Brussels: Commission of the European Communities.

1989e    *Directive 89/391/EEC on the introduction of measures to encourage improvement in the health and safety of workers.* Brussels: Commission of the European Communities.

1989f    *Directive 89/C263/01 on a general system for the mutual recognition of higher education diplomas awarded on completion of professional education and training of at least three years duration.* Brussels: Commission of the European Communities.

1989g    *Directive on the minimum health and safety requirements for the use by workers of personal protection equipment at the work place.* Third individual directive within the meaning of Article 16(1) of Directive 89/391/EEC. Brussels: Commission of the European Communities.

1989h    *Directive on the minimum safety and health requirements for work with display screen equipment.* Fifth individual directive within the meaning of Article 15(a) of Directive 87/391/EEC. Brussels: Commission of the European Communities.

1989i    *Directive 89/48/EEC to provide for the recognition of higher education diplomas awarded for occupations having a minimum training program of three years.* Brussels: Commission of the European Communities.

1989j    *Education and training in the European Community: Guidelines for the medium term, 1989-1992* COM (89) 236 Final. Brussels: Commission of the European Communities.

1989k    *Employment in Europe, 1989.* Brussels: Commission of the European Communities.

1989l    Employment in Europe. *Information Memo.* Brussels: Commission of the European Communities (July 5).

1989m    *European economy.*

1989n    *Fourth progress report of the Commission to the Council and the European Parliament* COM (89) 311 Final. Brussels: Commission of the European Communities.

1989o    *International Conference for Occupational Health, Safety and Hygiene Information Specialists* EUR 12560. Luxembourg, June 26–28.

1989p    Labour force survey 1987. *EUROSTAT Series.* Luxembourg: Office of Official Publications.

1989q    *Proposal for a Council directive complementing the Statute for a European Company with regard to the involvement of employees in the European Company* COM (89) 268 Final - SYN 219. Brussels: Commission of the European Communities.

1989r    *Proposal for a Council regulation on the Statute for a European Company* COM (89) 268 Final - SYN 218. Brussels: Commission of the European Communities.

1989s    *Proposal for a directive on voting rights for community nationals in local elections in their member state of residence* COM (89) 524 Final. Brussels: Commission of the European Communities.

1989t    *Social dimension of the internal market,* V/1264/89. Speech presented by Vasso Papandreou at the U.K. Trade Union Congress.

1989u    *Summary report on the comparative study on rules governing working conditions in the member states* SEC (89) 926 Final. Brussels: Commission of the European Communities.

1989v    The social aspects of the internal market. *Social Europe,* Vol. II, Supplement 7.

1989w    *Women of Europe,* 30. The Women's Information Service in DG X.

1990a    An expert's report on immigration policies and the social integration of immigrants in the European Community. *Information Memo.* Brussels: Commission of the European Communities (September 27).

1990b    The Commission proposes a directive on information and consultation of employees. *Information Memo.* Brussels: Commission of the European Communities (December 5).

1990c    *Employment in Europe, 1990.* Brussels: Commission of the European Communities.

1990d    Employment in Europe. *Information Memo.* Brussels: Commission of the European Communities, DG Employment, Industrial Relations, and Social Affairs.

1990e    *Eurobarometer,* Vol. 1 (no. 33, June).

1990f    Preliminary draft budget for 1991. *Information Memo.* Brussels: Commission of the European Communities (June 11).

1990g    *Social Europe*. Luxembourg: Office for Official Publications of the EC (July 15).

1990h    Special forms of employment. *Information Memo*. Brussels: Commission of the European Communities.

1990i    *Target '92* Supplement (no. 9). Brussels: Commission of the European Communities.

1990j    *Trade union information bulletin*, Vol. 1, 1990. Brussels: Trade Union Division of the Directorate General for Information, Communications and Culture.

1990k    *Travail Atypique*. Communication from Vasso Papandreou COM (90) 228/2. Brussels: Commission of the European Communities. [Contains drafts from the proposed directives on conditions of work, distortion of competition, and health and safety of temporary workers.]

1990l    *Women of Europe* (no. 31, August). The Women's Information Service in DG X.

1990m    *XXIIIrd general report on the activities of the European Communities 1989*. Brussels: Commission of the European Communities.

Cecchini, P.
1988    *The European challenge 1992*. Aldershot: Wildwood House.

CEDEFOP (European Centre for the Development of Vocational Training)
1989    *CEDEFOP Flash*. Berlin: European Centre for the Development of Vocational Training (February).

Chalude, M.
1982    *Women and job desegregation in banking*, V/2778/82. Brussels: Commission of the European Communities.

Corbett, R.
1989    Testing the new procedures: The European Parliament's first experiences with the new "Single Act" powers. *Journal of Common Market Studies*, 27 (no. 4, June): 359–372.

CREW (Centre for Research on European Women)
1989    *CREW reports*. Brussels: Centre for Research on European Women (Sept/Oct).

1990a    *CREW reports*. Brussels: Centre for Research on European Women (June/July).

1990b    *CREW reports*. Brussels: Centre for Research on European Women (Oct/Nov).

Dankert, P., and A. Kooyman, eds.
1989    *Europe without frontiers*. London: Mansell Publishing.

de Bassompierre, G.
1988    *Changing the guard in Brussels*. New York: Praeger.

December Council Meeting
1989     *European Industrial Relations Review*, Vol. 181 (February): 10-11.

Delors, J.
1988     1992: The social dimension. Address by Jacques Delors, Bournemouth, United Kingdom September 8.

Department of Labour, The
1990     *Women and the completion of the internal market: Report of a seminar organized by The Department of Labour, Dublin, and the Commission for the EC.* Dublin: The Department of Labour.

Economic and Social Committee
1989     *Basic community social rights: Opinion* CES 279/89 (February 22).

1990     Economic and Social Committee. *Opinion on the proposal for a Council regulation (EEC) on the Statute for a European Company and the proposal for a Council directive complementing the Statute for a European Company with regard to the involvement of employees in the European Company* CES 379/89 - SYN 218/SYN 219 (March 28). Brussels: European Parliament of the European Communities.

EFILWC (European Foundation for the Improvement of Living and Working Conditions)
1988     *New Forms of Work.* Dublin: European Foundation for the Improvement of Living and Working Conditions.

Environmental Resources Limited
1990     The impact of the occupational health and safety legislation of the European Community in the development of legislation in the member states. *Social Europe*, 2/90: 9-11.

EP (European Parliament of the European Communities)
1988a     Committee on Legal Affairs and Citizens' Rights. *Working document on employee participation and consultation under the national laws of the EEC member states and under EEC adopted and proposed legislation, especially the proposed Council directive complementing the Statute for a European Company with regard to the involvement of employees in the European Company.* Rapporteur: Christine Oddy PE 136.297 (December 13).

1988b     Committee on Women's Rights. *Working document on the effects of completion of the internal market in 1992.* Rapporteur: Mrs. M. van Hemeldonck, PE 126.971 (August 24).

1988c     *Dossier on the social dimension of the internal market* PE 119.003 (January).

1989a     *Resolution on the social dimension of the internal market* DOC A2-399/88 (March 15).

1989b   *Texts adopted by the European Parliament* (March, Second Parliamentary Term).

1990    Committee on Legal Affairs and Citizens' Rights. *Draft report on the proposal for a regulation on the Statute for a European Company* PE 139.411 (June 27).

ETUC (European Trade Union Confederation)
1983    *Report on activities: 1979-1982*. Brussels: European Trade Union Confederation.

1988a   *Community charter of social rights*. A report by the Executive Committee (December 1-2).

1988b   *Sixth Statutory Congress report on activities 85/87*. Brussels: European Trade Union Institute.

European Council
1990    *Presidency conclusions* SN 424/1/90. Rome: European Council (December 14 & 15).

France
1984    Law 83-635 of July 13, 1983 to modify the code of work and the penal code as it concerns professional equality between women and men. *Official Journal of the French Republic* (February 1): 487.

Gill, C.
1990    *Participation in new technology in the twelve member states of the European Community*, 12/90. Management Studies Research Paper. Cambridge, England: University of Cambridge.

Haas, E.
1964    *Beyond the nation state*. Stanford, CA: Stanford University Press.

1966    International integration: The European and the universal process. Chapter 10 in *International Political Communities*. New York: Doubleday & Co.

Institute of Personnel Management
1988    1992: Personnel management and the single European market. *European Report*. London: Institute of Personnel Management (October).

Jackson, P. C.
1989    *The impact of 1992 on women in the labour market*, V/1265/89. Brussels: Commission of the European Communities.

1990    *The impact of the completion of the internal market on women in the European Community*. A working document on the completion of the internal market and women in the European Community, V/506/90. Brussels: Commission of the European Communities.

Kirchner, E., and K. Williams
1983     The legal, political, and institutional implications of the Isoglucose
         Judgment 1980. *Journal of Common Market Studies*, 22 (no. 2,
         December).

Landau, E. C.
1985     *The rights of working women in the European Community.* Brussels:
         The European Perspective Series of the European Community.

Lasok, D., and J. W. Bridge
1987     *Law and institutions of the European Communities.* 4th ed. London:
         Butterworths.

Laufer, J.
1982     *Equal opportunity in banking in the countries of the EEC,*
         V/2455/1/82. Brussels: Commission of the European Communities.

Lawrence, P.
1980     *Managers and management in West Germany.* New York: St.
         Martin's Press.

Lodge, J., ed.
1989     *The European Community to the challenge of the future.* New York:
         St. Martin's Press.

Mazey, S.
1988     European Community actions on behalf of women: The limits of
         legislation. *Journal of Common Market Studies*, 27 (no. 1, Septem-
         ber): 63-84.

Miller, M. J.
1981     *Foreign workers in Western Europe.* New York: Praeger.

Molle, W.
1988     Regional policy. *Main economic policy areas of the EEC—Toward
         1992.* 2d rev. ed. Peter Coffey, ed. Boston: Kluwer Academic Press.

Molle, W., and R. Cappellin, eds.
1988     *Regional impact of community policies in Europe.* Aldershot, En-
         gland: Gower Publishing Company.

Mortensen, P.
1990     *The European company: Can it be realized?* [Unpublished manu-
         script.] (November 13).

Mowat, R. C.
1973     *Creating the European Community.* New York: Barnes & Noble.

Mutimer, D.
1989     1992 and the political integration of Europe: Neofunctionalism re-
         considered. *Journal of European Integration*, 13 (no. 1, Fall): 75-
         101.

OECD (Organization for Economic Cooperation and Development)
1985    *The integration of women into the economy.* Paris: Organization for
        Economic Cooperation and Development.

Padoa-Schioppa, T.
1987    *Efficiency, stability and equity.* Oxford: Oxford University Press.

Palmer, M.
1981    *The European Parliament: What it is, what it does, how it works.*
        Oxford: Pergamon Press.

Passionate Dimension, The
1989    *Economist* (April 8): 56.

Pe, J.
1989    Europe: Compler le vide social. *Force Ouvrière Hebdo* [official
        organ of the French CGT-FO] (March 22).

Peel, J.
1979    *The real power game.* London: McGraw-Hill.

Pryce, R., ed.
1987    *Dynamics of European union.* London: Croom Helm.

Quelch, J. A., and R. D. Buzzell
1990    *The marketing challenge of Europe 1992.* 2d ed. Reading, MA:
        Addison Wesley Publishing Co.

Seche, J. C.
1988    *A guide to working in a Europe without frontiers.* Brussels: Commis-
        sion of the European Communities.

Springer, B.
1987    The European Parliament: The quest for institutional balance. *The
        European Studies Journal,* IV (no. 1): 34–48.

Taylor, P.
1983    *The limits of European integration.* New York: Columbia University
        Press.

Teague, P.
1989    *The European Community: The social dimension.* London: Kogan
        Page.

Tyszkiewicz, Z.J.A.
1989    Employers' views in the Community Charter of Basic Social Rights
        for Workers. *Social Europe* 1/90: 22–24.

U.K. Trade Union Congress
1988    Maximising the benefits: Minimising the costs. *TUC Report on
        Europe 1992* (August). London: U.K. Trade Union Congress.

UNICE
1976    Employee participation and company structure. [Mimeographed
        paper dated June 3.]

1981    *Press release.* (February 20).

1988a   *The social dimension of the internal market.*

1988b   *L'achévement du Marché intévieur à mi-parcous: Position de l'UNICE.* (October 3).

von Prondzynski, F., ed.

1990    *Women and the completion of the internal market.* Dublin: The Department of Labour, Ireland.

Williams, R., M. Teagan, and J. Beneyto.

1990    *The world's largest market: A business guide to Europe 1992.* New York: AMACOM.

# Index

## About the Author

BEVERLY SPRINGER is Professor of International Studies at Thunderbird—the American Graduate School of International Management and the author of several articles.